Praise for Conversations About Race

Common Ground
"The theme of this book is our shared humanity. Marjy Marj seeks to illuminate the ties that bind us regardless of the many differences among us. She aims to find those common denominators and use them as building blocks toward empathy and understanding, with an eye toward expanding people's lenses. The author seems to say, Let's celebrate our differences as they are the spice of life, while also acknowledging that we are more alike than different. What dehumanizes one, dehumanizes all. Building up is way better than breaking down."
-- Michel Stone, Author, *Border Child*

A Great Read
"I love how the author used her experience with others to show how we can find value in each other. I especially like the Reflections section. It gives you a pause to think about what is being discussed, and how you can become a part of the solution with humanity."
 -- Dr. Eliza Osae-Kwapong

Tough Conversation Book
"This book touches the very heart of what's needed to start a conversation about race and the reason there needs to be a conversation."
-- Hope Blackley, Former Clerk of Court and Contributor, Conversations About Race

Thoughtful Conversation Starter
"It is very approachable and a great launching point for discussions of race. On a personal note, this book helped me to start seeing what other people have experienced in their lives. The questions let me look at myself and my assumptions. Read this ... and then read it again."
-- Susan Myers, Librarian

Conversations About Race

Humanity Chats

MARJY MARJ

CONVERSATIONS ABOUT RACE

For Humanity

To: Sarah.

Together, we
can go far!

Majy Mz

CONVERSATIONS ABOUT RACE

This book is for all of us.

Our small actions can create a movement for good.

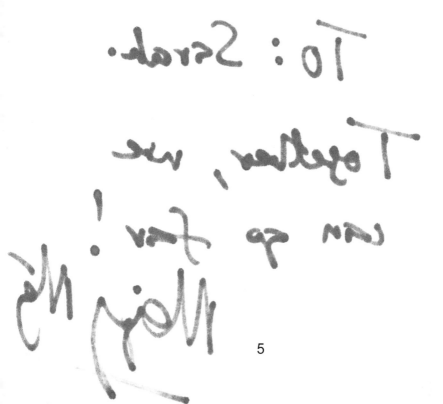

CONVERSATIONS ABOUT RACE

Table of Contents

Why I Wrote this Book
Different but Similar
Race
Xenophobia
Colorism
Yellow Peril and Asian Hate
Hispanic Heritage
Broadening Our Lens
Racial Inequality
Creating Racially Equitable Systems
Education
Mentorship and Community
Perspective
Empathy
Faith
Unity
Inclusion and Belonging
The New Normal
The Way Forward
Acknowledgements
About the Author
Other Books by the Author

Note

Please note that conversations with guests have been italicized.

Why I Wrote this Book

Why I Wrote this Book

Race conversations can sometimes be difficult and even emotionally charged. Yet, these discussions, as uncomfortable as they can be, hold an undeniable importance in our lives. I've learned firsthand that the willingness to delve into these dialogues, to truly understand each other's experiences and perspectives, can be a powerful tool. It has helped me to bolster relationships that could've easily slipped through the cracks, as a result of misunderstanding or a lack of communication. The benefits of engaging in these dialogues far outweigh any discomfort they may cause.

By choosing to listen, to learn, and to engage, we can transform the awkward, often difficult conversations into bridges connecting us, making us stronger as individuals and as a collective. These conversations are essential because they allow us to challenge our assumptions and beliefs, learn from one another's experiences, and ultimately work towards a more equitable and just society. They also provide an opportunity for us to examine our own biases and privilege, as well as those of others.

As a black Ghanaian-American woman, my perspective on race has evolved over the years. Being born and raised in Ghana, race, as a concept, was quite straightforward during my formative years. Unlike the diverse racial landscape that I would later encounter in America, everyone around me was black. This homogeneity, in many ways, simplified the idea of race in my early life. I was able to view myself and others through a lens untainted by racial prejudice. However, I cannot be dismissive of the tribal and nationalistic lens with which I viewed others - a fact that I came to recognize later on in life.

My experiences in America challenged my simplistic understanding of race and forced me to confront the complexities and consequences of racial discrimination. As I navigated through spaces where my race was seen as a defining aspect of my identity, I began to understand the weight and impact of systemic racism on individuals and communities.

However, it was not until I engaged in meaningful and open dialogues with people of different racial backgrounds that I truly grasped the importance of these conversations. Through listening to others' perspectives and sharing my own, I was able to expand my understanding and uncover blind spots in my thinking.

These conversations were not always easy. They forced me to confront uncomfortable truths about myself. But through them, I was able to break down barriers and build bridges with individuals who were different from me.

I believe that open and honest conversations about race are crucial for creating a more inclusive and just society. They provide an opportunity for us to learn from one another, challenge harmful stereotypes, and promote empathy and understanding. However, it's important to remember that these conversations should not fall solely on the shoulders of people of color.

During my formative years in Ghana, I found myself harboring a bias - a belief that white individuals were inherently superior, more intelligent, more significant. I wrestled with the origin of this perception, questioning whether it was an influence of the media, with its frequent depiction of white characters in dominant, successful roles, or if it was a result of internalized colonial mentality.

I found this bias reflected in everyday encounters. For instance, at the local market, the traders would extend preferential treatment towards white customers, an implicit validation of the notion that being white equates to being better.

In Ghana, historical narratives had introduced me to the concept of slavery, a cruel chapter of human history. However, it wasn't until my relocation to America that the full weight of its legacy truly hit me. My perspective began to shift. I started to see the systemic issues of racism and privilege that exist in our global society, and how they perpetuate harmful beliefs and attitudes towards people of color. My own experiences as an immigrant further solidified this understanding.

These realizations have sparked a desire within me to initiate and participate in more conversations about race and diversity. I believe that it's through these discussions that we can begin to break down the barriers that divide us and build bridges of understanding. As a society, we must be willing to engage in uncomfortable conversations and challenge our own biases and assumptions.

As I became more aware of the stark realities of racial disparities. I saw how the color of one's skin dramatically influenced perceptions, often leading to unwarranted accusations and disproportionate charges for crimes committed. This wasn't simply an issue of individual bias, but a societal structure that perpetuated certain perceptions. As I navigated my own experiences as a black immigrant, these insights fueled my determination to engage in conversations about race, aiming to listen to and learn from different voices.

An experience that impacted my decision to delve deeper into race conversations was a visit to Ghana in the early 2000s. Returning to the slave dungeons in Ghana with my American-born son was an experience that was profound and heartrending. As I observed the lines etched on the dungeon walls, a stark reminder of our ancestors' suffering, I had goosebumps. The lines created from the dried feces, a grim testament to the inhuman conditions they were subjected to, left an indelible mark on me. My heart ached and I couldn't hold back my tears when our guide pointed out the trap doors through which females were transported to be raped. Vivid images flooded my mind as I imagined their screams, their tears, and their unbearable pain. This visit was a stark reminder of the unspeakable horrors endured by those who came before us.

I felt a profound sense of betrayal. Why were our people so quick to turn on each other? Why did we help the colonizer capture our own? I had so many questions, each one a painful reminder of our past. The existence of such treachery within our own African community made me uneasy.

But despite the painful history, I also saw resilience and hope. As we stopped at the Door of No Return, I reminded myself that our ancestors who passed through that door were the ancestors of great inventors and trailblazers. Their descendants such as the great Dr. Martin Luther King, have their names etched in history.

To my brothers and sisters whose ancestors had to make the treacherous journey across the ocean to be enslaved, I am truly sorry. Your ancestors were stripped of their dignity, their freedom, and their lives. The echoes of their pain reverberate through the annals of our shared history, a grim reminder of man's inhumanity to man. The strength and resilience they demonstrated, however, is nothing short of inspirational. They endured, they adapted, and they laid the foundation for the liberties and opportunities we relish today.

To the people of African descent: We are one heritage, one people. The blood that courses through our veins carries with it the legacy of our forebears, the echoes of their triumphs and their sorrows. It is up to us to honor their memory, to ensure that their sacrifices were not in vain. We are the dream and the hope of the slaves, the fulfillment of their aspirations.

Together, we can create a better world for all of us. Therefore, let us strive to build bridges, not walls, to foster understanding and empathy, not disdain and discord. Let us rise above the divisions of the past, the prejudices, and unite in our common humanity.

As a resident of America, I couldn't help but notice that several positions of power lacked representation from people who looked like me. Coming from a country where black judges serve on the supreme court, where we had Black Presidents, and professionals of all stripes who looked like me, the stark contrast was glaring. The lack of diversity in power positions was palpable, and the underrepresentation unsettling.

However, then came a glimmer of hope, a moment of profound significance – the election of President Barack Obama, America's first Black President. This was a milestone, a historic moment that signaled a shift in America's political landscape. It was a testament to the progress we have made as a nation, a beacon of hope for future generations. It signaled that the impenetrable barriers, the glass ceilings, could indeed be shattered. It was a moment of celebration, not just for Black Americans, but for all who believe in equality, diversity, and representation. The significance of President Obama's election was more than a political victory, it was a validation of our ancestors' dreams and aspirations.

This monumental event marked a turning point in American politics and society. It showed that progress towards diversity and representation was not just a dream, but a tangible reality. However, it also highlighted the work that still needs to be done. While President Obama's election was a step forward, it also brought attention to the lack of diversity in other areas of power and influence.

The need for equitable representation in all levels of government, business, and society became even more apparent. The conversation around diversity and inclusion gained momentum, with calls for action to address systemic barriers and create a more inclusive society.

The election of President Obama also showed the power of representation and visibility. For many young Black Americans, seeing someone who looked like them in the highest position of political power was a source of inspiration and motivation. It showed that anything is possible, regardless of race or background. Representation matters, and the impact of seeing oneself reflected in positions of influence cannot be underestimated.

Reflecting on the accomplishments of several inspiring individuals, I am filled with a deep sense of pride and admiration. The Late General Colin Powell, a man of leadership and integrity, demonstrated that excellence transcends racial boundaries. His journey, from humble beginnings to becoming America's top military officer and later Secretary of State, reinforces the belief that with determination and hard work, one can break glass ceilings.

The rise of Madam Condoleezza Rice to Secretary of State, the first African-American woman to hold this position, was an affirmation of the capabilities and resilience of Black women. Her contributions to foreign policy, defense strategies, and national security act as a testament to her intellect and acumen, proving that women are making significant strides in a world previously dominated by men.

The election of Vice President Kamala Harris, a woman of South Asian and African American descent, was a moment of immense jubilation. It brought forth a sense of belonging and representation for millions of marginalized people. On her inauguration day, I, like many others, wore pearls to honor her achievement. It was a symbol of solidarity and a celebration of diversity and representation in the highest echelons of politics.

Moreover, the celebration of Diwali at the White House, a sign of acceptance and respect towards the Indian-American community, was beautiful to behold. It portrayed a multicultural America that welcomed the traditions and customs of all its citizens, demonstrating the richness of its cultural tapestry.

The recent appointments of Dr. Claudine Gay and Justice Ketanji Brown Jackson further amplified the feeling of pride. Dr. Gay, as the first female Black President of Harvard University, shattered a historical glass ceiling in academia. Justice Jackson, as the first Black woman to serve on the Supreme Court, brings a fresh perspective and a much-needed voice to a powerful institution. Their stories are an inspiration for future generations, proving once again that race or gender should not be a barrier to achieving one's dreams.

Although the journey is far from over, recent victories for marginalized communities in First World countries inspire hope and promise a brighter future. These accomplishments are a testament to the spirit of perseverance and resilience that these communities embody. Every victory, every shattered glass ceiling, every barrier overcome, resonates powerfully within these communities, fostering a sense of empowerment and reinforcing the belief that they, too, can reach the heights of success.

These strides forward are not just steps towards equality, but monumental leaps towards a future where every individual, regardless of their race, gender, or religion, is given an equal platform to actualize their dreams. The narrative of minorities thriving in First World countries is not just about the individuals' triumph; it is a celebration of the collective perseverance and efforts. This narrative serves as a beacon guiding us towards a future where diversity and representation are celebrated and valued.

As I reflect upon history, I am particularly moved by the inspiring stories of stalwarts like President Kwame Nkrumah, Rosa Parks, and Dr. Martin Luther King Jr.

Nkrumah, who led Ghana to independence from colonial rule, was a beacon of hope not just for his country but for all of Africa. His vision of Pan-Africanism, advocating for a united Africa capable of self-governance, continues to inspire leaders today.

Rosa Parks, by refusing to surrender her seat to a white passenger on a segregated bus, became an enduring symbol of the Civil Rights Movement. Her courageous act of defiance in the face of oppressive laws sparked a wave of protests that ultimately led to the end of segregation on public transportation. Her strength and determination serve as a clear reminder of the power of standing firm in one's convictions.

Dr. Martin Luther King Jr., a central figure in the American civil rights movement, championed the cause of racial equality through nonviolent resistance. His powerful speeches and peaceful protests played a pivotal role in the passing of the Civil Rights Act of 1964 and the Voting Rights Act of 1965. His legacy, encapsulated in his famous "I Have a Dream" speech, continues to resonate with humans around the world.

These individuals, along with countless unnamed heroes, dared to challenge the status quo, sparking pivotal conversations about race, independence, and progress. They faced immense adversity with courage and resilience, transforming society for the better.

As we continue to benefit from their collective efforts, it is our responsibility to honor their legacy by continuing the dialogue on these critical issues and striving for a more equitable world.

Without these advocates, some of us may not have had the opportunity to attend certain schools, let alone aspire to lofty academic and career ambitions. It is due to their relentless pursuit of justice and equality that we enjoy the liberties and opportunities that we sometimes take for granted today. Their tireless efforts paved the way for desegregation of schools, making education an equal right and not a privilege skewed by race or socioeconomic status.

Can we imagine a world in which we were barred from riding on the same buses due to the color of our skin? The thought seems ludicrous now, but it was a reality not too long ago. It was the unyielding resolve of advocates - both black and white, that brought an end to such discriminatory practices, promoting unity and equality in all spheres of public life.

The right to vote, a fundamental tenet of any democratic society, was also a hard-fought victory. People of color in the United States, once denied this crucial civil right, can now participate fully and freely in the electoral process. This change was not brought about overnight – it was the result of decades of struggle, protest, and advocacy.

These historical milestones, achieved through the courage and determination of advocates for equality, remind us that change and transformation is possible. The narrative of progress, particularly in First World countries, is a testament to this principle. It is a narrative that is continuously being written, with each new victory serving as a fresh chapter in an unfolding saga of resilience, endurance, and hope for a better future.

However, as we celebrate historic moments and progress, it is important to acknowledge the challenges that still exist. As citizens of the world, we must do our best to advocate for each other. Inclusion, respect, and fairness should be the foundational ideals of our global community.

Advocating for others includes fostering an environment that celebrates diversity, promotes mutual understanding, and facilitates equal opportunity. This understanding has taught me that welcoming others as well as providing equity and opportunity for others is a way of enhancing the value of our society.

When we strive to level the playing field for everyone, we are not just honoring the legacy of the changemakers who preceded us, but we are also creating a world that is more innovative, productive, and harmonious. By recognizing and dismantling the barriers faced by marginalized groups, we can foster a society where every individual has the potential to contribute their unique perspective and talent. This is the essence of adding value to society - the realization that in our diversity lies our strength. Our effort, therefore, should be directed towards cultivating and promoting this diversity.

As I assimilated and broadened my interactions in America, I came to realize that the Black community was not the only group striving for justice and equity. Individuals from various ethnicities and identities, be they of Asian descent, South American heritage, Native American roots, Native Hawaiian or Pacific Islander lineage, Alaska Natives, Middle Easterners, or Whites, are all striving towards the same goal. This also extends to people of different religious backgrounds and to the LGBTQ+ community.

Each of these groups, with their unique histories and experiences, face their own distinct set of challenges in their pursuit of equal opportunities. This realization has deepened my commitment to advocacy. It is evident that the pursuit of a fair society is not just the struggle of one community but a collective responsibility. Through mutual understanding and respect, we can break down the barriers that hinder us and together, create a society that values humans.

As you are probably aware, discrimination does not pertain to just one race. It does not even pertain to just one culture. It has permeated every facet of our society, becoming an unseen force that shapes the experiences and opportunities of countless individuals. Discrimination, in its many forms, is a pervasive issue, cutting across racial, ethnic, religious, and gender lines. It manifests in a myriad of ways - from subtle microaggressions and unconscious bias to outright hate speech and violence.

Discrimination, while deeply embedded in our society, is not an unchangeable aspect of our culture. Through conversations, open dialogue, education, advocacy, and policy reforms, we can challenge the systemic inequities that persist and strive for a society where every individual is treated with dignity and respect. As we continue this journey towards inclusivity, it is paramount that we continue advocating for the rights and equal treatment of the members of our society.

I'll admit it, I'm not exempt from the flaws I've discussed above. I don't know about you, but I have the tendency to put individuals in boxes, seeing them through the lens of simplified, preconceived categorizations. Yes, I am guilty of stereotyping. It's a hard admission, but a necessary one. More often than not, I find myself needing to take a step back, to remind myself of the complexity and individuality of each person I encounter. I need to remember to see the bigger picture, to see people for who they truly are - not just the labels society has attached to them.

This admission brings me to the crux of why I wrote this book. It's not just an account for you, the reader, but a personal journey for myself as well. Writing out my thoughts, confessing my shortcomings, exploring the impact of discrimination, and charting a path towards inclusivity has been a therapeutic process. It's been a mirror reflecting back my own conditioned biases, a tool for self-reflection, growth, and hopefully, change.

Through this book, I hope to take a step closer towards a more inclusive mindset, and I invite you to join me in this journey.

The genesis of this book can be traced back to my previous work "Same Elephants," a fictional narrative published in 2020. The story revolves around four friends, each hailing from distinctive backgrounds, who manage to transcend their differences to form a bond of friendship. This endeavor was not just a simple portrayal of friendship but also a deliberate attempt to ignite conversations about race.

The book commences with a poem titled "The Human Oath," which encapsulates the essence of the narrative. The oath goes as follows:

> We are humans
> From all around the world
> One kind only
> And that is humankind

This verse is a testament to the underlying theme of this book: embracing our shared humanity. It set the tone for the story, inviting readers to reflect on the unity that lies beneath our apparent differences. As we delve deeper into the topic of inclusivity in the following chapters of this book, the ethos of "The Human Oath" will serve as our guiding principle.

In April 2020, as I sat in isolation during the Covid-19 pandemic, I picked up "Same Elephants" and started reading it aloud. The tears were streaming down my face. I could relate to the characters in the book. I felt their joy and their pain. When I got to the part where two of the four girls were accused of trespassing, I was overwhelmed with empathy, picturing myself in the same dire predicament.

I was reminded of an evening when I was mistaken for a trespasser in my own neighborhood. My immediate reaction to being mistaken for a trespasser was not pleasant. Not only was I livid, I was also quick to accuse and insult the perpetrators. No, I did not execute the calm responses that I had taught myself. My response to the situation brought forth a question that had been lingering in the back of my mind for a long time: would it ever be possible for us to put our differences aside and live in harmony? Could we overcome our inherent biases?

Then I had an idea, why don't I host a group chat about humanity, where we could candidly discuss the everyday issues that impact us? That evening, we initiated our first "Humanity Chat" on Instagram Live. My initial thought was to organize a few sessions, using the platform to highlight human interest stories and engage in meaningful discussions. Before we knew it, one conversation naturally evolved into the next.

Over time, these discussions have grown and deepened, encompassing a broad range of topics that go beyond the surface level. We've delved into subjects such as colorism, xenophobia, and racial inequities, fostering a space for open dialogue and mutual learning. From those humble beginnings, our "Humanity Chat" has come a long way, and our journey continues.

The "Humanity Chats" have evolved into a haven for many, providing solace and understanding. In the aftermath of the tragic demise of George Floyd and the subsequent racial protests that swept the nation, people from all walks of life converged in our virtual space. They shared their thoughts, fears, hopes, and insights, tackling the complex issue of race and its profound implications on society.

This book seeks to encapsulate some of those poignant discussions, offering a glimpse into the raw, unfiltered emotions and perspectives emanating from these chats. As we journey through the chapters, readers will have the opportunity to experience the authenticity of these conversations, bearing witness to the healing and transformative power of dialogue.

As a result of the rich diversity and gravity of topics discussed on "Humanity Chats", the platform attracted a mosaic of individuals from different socio-economic and educational backgrounds. Christians, Muslims, Republicans, Democrats, Blacks, Whites, Browns - people from all walks of life, spanning more than 1,000 cities, convened in these virtual spaces. Every session was a microcosm of our global society, a blend of thoughts and perspectives, that were as diverse as they were unified in their quest for truth.

There were days when the dialogues were imbued with a palpable sense of optimism, the virtual room buzzing with the energy of potential solutions and bridge-building. Yet, there were occasions when closure was elusive, days when the conversations ended with a collective sigh, a quiet acknowledgment of the depth and complexity of the issues being tackled.

These were difficult conversations, indeed, yet their necessity was never in question. In many ways, these challenging discussions served as a reflection of the real-world dialogues happening every day. They underscored the importance of open, honest conversation in our journey toward mutual understanding and societal harmony.

The discussions, although daunting, inspired me to further explore the contours of inclusivity, leading to the creation of this book. I hope that through these pages, we can find some answers together.

In the following chapters, we will delve into topics that shape our perception of others. We will also discuss methods for fostering empathy and understanding among individuals from diverse backgrounds. We will share about actively welcoming and embracing our humanity and diversity. This mindset shift is necessary for creating community.

Through my own experiences and continued education, I have come to understand that conversations about race and diversity are not just limited to the past. They are ongoing discussions that need to be had in order for us to move forward as a society. We must acknowledge the systemic structures that continue to perpetuate disharmony and actively work towards dismantling them.

As I embarked on this journey to share my thoughts and experiences, I realized that it wasn't going to be a smooth ride. Writing this book has not been an easy task. I found myself questioning the necessity of it, given the vast amount of literature, movements, and dialogues already existing around the subject of race. Yet, every time I asked myself, "Is it really necessary to have yet another discussion on race?", my answer was a resounding yes.

I do not claim to be an expert on race relations, nor do I have all the answers to the complex questions that arise when we delve into this topic. My understanding is based on my experiences, and the wisdom gained through them. However, I believe that if my experiences, my stories, and my insights can touch even a single person, can make even a small positive impact, then I am willing to share. For it is through sharing our experiences and learning from each other that we can hope to foster understanding, empathy, and ultimately, change.

So, as we continue on this journey together, I invite you to join me with an open mind and heart. Let us challenge the status quo and strive towards creating a community of love - regardless of race, ethnicity, gender, or any other factor that society has used to divide us. Let us have difficult conversations and listen to different voices.

This book encapsulates the personal experiences and the shared knowledge of the dedicated guests who joined our Humanity Chats to discuss race-related issues from April 2020 to October 2022. However, it is important to remember that these conversations are profoundly filtered through our personal perspectives and experiences. We are, after all, limited by the confines of an introductory book and we are unable to delve into much deeper and complex conversations. Even so, the aim has always been clear – to broaden your lens, to promote understanding, and to inspire action.

My sincere hope is that by the time you turn the last page of this book, you will not only be more aware of the complexities of race relations but also feel compelled to join us in moving the unity needle forward. Remember, we are in this together, and together, we can go far.

Thank you for embarking on this journey with me. Let us build bridges instead of walls, break down barriers instead of creating them, and work towards a society where diversity is celebrated, and equality is the norm. Our differences should not divide us, but rather unite us in our shared humanity. Together, we can make this vision a reality.

Your Friend,

Marjy Marj

Different but Similar

Different but Similar

"Different but similar" is a phrase that captures the essence of our shared humanity. Despite our varying backgrounds, cultures, and experiences, we are all part of the human race. We share a universal need for connection, understanding, and mutual respect.

There is a popular proverb that says, "A friend in need is a friend indeed." It underscores the importance of showing up for others during their times of need, an act that transcends all differences. It is a simple yet profound statement about human relationships. It doesn't matter where we come from, what language we speak, or what color our skin is. When we face challenges, we turn to those who are there for us.

To demonstrate the power of friendship and solidarity, I'd like to share stories about my friends Ansley and John. These stories explore the bonds that hold us together despite our apparent differences.

Ansley is a white woman from South Carolina. Despite our different backgrounds, we share the same faith. As I was preparing for major surgery, she stepped in and proved the proverb "A friend in need is a friend indeed."

On the morning of my surgery, Ansley was one of the first people to make it to the pre-op area. As she stood in silence, she reached out for my hand and began praying for me. A fervent prayer for strength and healing.

She could sense my anxiety as my eyes glistened with tears. Ansley rubbed my hands, tightened her grip on my hand, leaned in closer, and whispered "You are going to be okay."

Her words, coupled with the comforting pressure of her hand, brought me comfort. As I looked around, I was touched by the care emanating from everyone in the room — my doctors, my family, my pastor... Their collective presence helped to replace the fear with a sense of reassurance.

Days later, after I was discharged from the hospital, Ansley sat at my bedside at home -

her presence as reliable as ever. Her attention was unwavering. She brought my favorite lavender lotion, a prayer shawl wrapped with hope, and a myriad of tiny delights that warmed my heart.

Her empathy was noticeable. She would hold a glass of water, her eyes pleading with me to take even the smallest sip. In the moments when I needed to throw up, she was swift to provide a bowl, never flinching, always supportive.

During my time of need, Ansley was more than a friend; she was a sister. Like the rest of us, she isn't without her flaws, but what sets her apart is her willingness to take care of her fellow humans. Also, she is willing to learn, to listen, and to grow. For that, I am profoundly grateful.

Now, let me pivot to John. A New York Times bestselling author, John's work has been acknowledged by former Vice President Mike Pence. Enamored by President Abraham Lincoln, John wrote a historical novel titled "Old Abe".

Despite our differences, John remains supportive of my work. For example, during the launch of my first book, John didn't simply send a congratulatory text or make a quick phone call; he went above and beyond. He took it upon himself to invite an impressive ensemble of guests to my book launch, ensuring that the room was at capacity.

On the day of the event, John was one of the first to arrive, his face beaming with pride for his friend. His smile radiated throughout the room, filling me with a sense of accomplishment and gratitude. His relentless support spoke volumes - a friend who wants his friend to succeed.

Yet, even with our shared love for books, differences persist. There are moments when our opinions diverge so much that consensus seems impossible. However, I've come to understand that these differences, the disagreements, are not a sign of discord but rather a reflection of our unique experiences. The divergences of thought is indeed, what has shaped each of us into who we are.

In the grand scheme of life, it's our differences that make our friendship unique, a testament to the fact that unity can indeed coexist with diversity.

John's friendship, like Ansley's, is a testament to the fact that we can be different, yet similar.

Our diversity should be seen not as a divide, but as a rich tapestry that adds depth, and strength to our collective identity as humans.

Throughout the years, as my social network has grown, I've had the privilege of encountering individuals from varied racial backgrounds, diverse genders, and an array of political affiliations. Each acquaintance, each interaction has enriched me with fresh perspectives and unique life stories.

My friendship with Ansley and John has been enlightening. Despite the color of our skin, we all share a profound, unwavering love for our families. It's a shared sentiment that transcends our superficial differences, reminding us of our common humanity.

If I was to write about all my friends, acquaintances, and enemies, this book would be bigger than an encyclopedia. Each individual has their unique traits, their quirks, their attitudes, painting a vibrant spectrum of human behavior.

From these diverse interactions, a crucial lesson I have garnered is the intrinsic value in all of us, irrespective of our differences. Our contrasting appearances and thought processes merely skim the surface of our identities. In reality, when we take the time to delve deeper and truly understand one another, we unearth striking similarities that bind us together. In essence, our disparities are not divisive but rather, they enrich our collective experience.

In conclusion, I invite you to engage in some introspection, assessing how our shared experiences and diverse backgrounds influence our interactions and relationships. Reflecting on the questions that follow may shed light on our shared humanity and our capacity for empathy, understanding, and mutual respect.

Reflections:

1. What are some of the activities that you share in common with others who may appear different from you on the surface?

2. Would you be open to sharing a meal with someone who practices a different religion or upholds a different political ideology?

Race

Race

"Race is still lingering - It's crippling us - We have to be able to trust one another and be authentic." - Dr. Russell Booker

In this chapter, we share the pervasive influence of race on our societal structures, examining its various manifestations and how it continues to hinder our ability to trust one another and be authentic in our interactions.

Dr. Russell Booker's poignant words highlight a challenge in our society: the issue of race. Despite the strides we've made towards inclusivity and acceptance, race continues to be a divisive factor in certain spheres, casting a shadow over our interactions and relationships.

During our Humanity Chat with Dr. Russell Booker, a former school district superintendent, he offered profound insights on the continuing issue of race. Known for his candor and wisdom, Dr. Booker emphasized the persistent and crippling effects of racial divisions.

Dr. Booker passionately advocated for a period of introspection and self-examination, urging individuals to look inward and scrutinize their own hearts rather than focusing on the actions of others. At times, he shared his feelings of discouragement, pessimism, and jadedness resulting from the lingering issues of racial inequality. Yet, his hope for substantial progress within his lifetime remains undiminished.

Stressing the importance of trust and authenticity, Dr. Booker emphasized that a unifying voice is a powerful tool in addressing racial disparities. As per his perspective, the fight against racial inequality requires a symphony of diverse voices. This includes truth-tellers who confront reality head-on, individuals who refuse to accept the status quo, and decision-makers in boardrooms who can enact systemic changes.

Dr. Booker likened the race issue to cancer, a devastating plague that continues to afflict society. He encouraged the proactive approach of self-education through books and articles and the value of engaging in dialogues about race. In his opinion, such actions are instrumental in understanding and ultimately eradicating the racial disparities that continue to undermine our society.

This candid conversation with Dr. Booker encourages each one of us to reflect, take action, and contribute to the movement for racial equality.

For those in search of further enlightenment on race issues, Dr. Booker recommends James

Baldwin's book, "Nobody Knows My Name". This classic piece of literature offers invaluable perspectives that challenge and deepen our understanding of race and racism.

Dr. Booker passionately believes that to truly eliminate racism, we must appreciate humanity in all its diverse splendor. It is by recognizing and valuing our differences that we can cultivate an inclusive society where every voice is heard and respected. But inclusivity, as he emphasizes, is only the first step. He proposes that we must strive to foster a sense of belonging, a society where everyone's voice not only exists but is actively listened to and considered.

In Dr. Booker's words, "striving doesn't mean we have arrived, we will have to keep working toward progress - plans are not actions. If we don't implement it, it's just living in our heads."

This profound statement reinforces the importance of action. Constructing a vision for a more equal society is vital, but it remains a mere dream unless we commit to turning these plans into tangible actions.

As we continue this crucial journey towards racial equality, let us remember Dr. Booker's insightful words and strive to translate our aspirations into meaningful action.

Commentary:

I remember the day when my seven-year-old son shared an intriguing story about his white friend. His friend, he said with an innocent sparkle in his eyes, didn't realize he was black because he was "colorblind". I smiled. Patiently, I explained to him what colorblindness really meant, and that his friend did indeed know he was black.

I reassured him that he was cherished, not for the color of his skin, but for being himself. I told him how his talents were appreciated. I reminded him that he and his friend, despite their distinct skin colors, were both children of God, deserving of love and respect.

The memory of that conversation brings a warm smile to my face even today. Seeing the two boys together now, their friendship has grown from those naive elementary school days. They've come a long way, their bond a testament to their individual characters, not their race. Their friendship, a silent but powerful answer to the naivety of children when questions about race arise.

In retrospect, I wonder what my seven-year-old thought about the color of his skin at that early age. Why did he assume that being colorblind meant that his friend did not know his race?

Maybe his thought had nothing to do with race but rather the misconstrued meaning of the word colorblind. Or maybe he was keenly aware of his blackness in a predominantly white space. The innocence of his question revealed his understanding of a world where color often shapes perception. It was an insight into how he was processing his place and identity in a world that still grapples with our racial differences. Today, as the boys have grown and their understanding of the world has matured, I hope they both continue to see each other beyond the color of their skin, appreciating the strength of character and shared values.

When we ponder about the word "race", a myriad of thoughts and images may cross our minds. The Merriam Webster Dictionary defines it as "any one of the groups that humans are often divided into based on physical traits regarded as common among people of shared ancestry." This definition, while accurate, is merely a surface-level understanding of the concept. The idea of race extends beyond mere physical characteristics; it encompasses deeply ingrained societal constructs, historical contexts, and the shared experiences of individuals within racial groups. This deeper understanding, often overlooked, plays a significant role in shaping our identities, relationships, and interactions within society. As we navigate the complexities of race and its implications, it's crucial to remember the essence of humanity transcends these divisions, rooting firmly in the strength of our character and shared values.

Building upon this understanding, the Oxford Dictionary defines a racist as "a person who is prejudiced against or antagonistic toward people on the basis of their membership in a particular racial or ethnic group, typically one that is a minority or marginalized." This definition sheds light on the inherent biases and prejudices that fuel racism. Yet, it's crucial to note that this definition, like that of race, merely scratches the surface. Racism is not just individual prejudice; it is systemic and institutional, deeply embedded into the structures of our society. It affects access to resources, opportunities, and even affects the experiences and outcomes of individuals within those racial or ethnic groups. Recognizing and acknowledging the pervasive nature of racism is the first step towards dismantling it and moving towards a more inclusive and equitable society.

The definition of racism, as provided by the Oxford Dictionary, is undoubtedly substantial in providing the foundation for understanding this complex issue. Yet, it may not resonate with everyone due to its somewhat impersonal nature.

It's understandable if, as a reader, you find it uncomfortable to associate yourself with the label of 'racist.' This discomfort arises because we often view ourselves through the lens of our intentions, not necessarily our actions or the impact of those actions. However, it's critical to realize that many of us have at some point unintentionally perpetuated or contributed to racist practices or mindsets.

This isn't an indictment but an invitation to self-reflection. We must understand that racism is not only overt actions of discrimination but also the subtler, unconscious biases we carry. These are often a result of societal conditioning over time and may manifest in our words, attitudes, and actions without our awareness. Acknowledging this is not about attaching a label to ourselves, but rather about accepting our past mistakes and using them as a stepping stone towards personal growth and societal change.

Stereotypes, essentially over generalizations about a group of people, have a profound impact on our behaviors, often leading to prejudiced actions and responses. It's not unusual to react instinctively out of fear or mistrust, bred by these ingrained stereotypes.

Reflect on this – how many times have you clutched your purse a bit tighter or rolled up your car window due to the person approaching?

These reactions are not always rooted in personal experiences but often stem from societal stereotypes.

This isn't to say we don't ever catch ourselves in these moments. Many times, we do become conscious of our judgmental tendencies and manage to halt them. However, unfortunately, this isn't always the case. It's these unchecked biases that contribute to the sedimentation of racial and ethnic disparities in our society.

The key lies in constantly checking our biases, questioning our behaviors and beliefs, and challenging the stereotypes that influence them. By doing so, we can gradually dismantle these harmful preconceptions and make strides towards a more inclusive society.

As a black woman, this harsh reality applies even to my family. I constantly remind the males in my household not to wear hoodies when they go jogging, a seemingly innocuous choice of clothing. However, this advice is rooted in the painful lessons learned from the tragic circumstances involving Trayvon Martin and Ahmaud Arbery. These instances serve as stark reminders that our society continues to grapple with deep-seated racial prejudices.

These prejudices persistently seep into our day-to-day lives, influencing how we perceive and react to others based on their race or the color of their skin. And these biases aren't always evident in monumental, headline-grabbing events but are often observed in subtle ways -- prejudiced gazes, hushed whispers, and unwarranted suspicion. It's a constant struggle against an unseen opponent, one that cloaks itself in the guise of 'normal' behaviors and societal norms.

This, unfortunately, is the reality for many black individuals and families, a reality that we must acknowledge and confront. It is through this acknowledgment and understanding that we can begin to break down these barriers, and move toward a society where the color of one's skin or their choice of clothing doesn't determine their safety or how they're perceived by others.

The conversations within black families often involve more than just the usual parental advice. We find ourselves advising our young black men not to put their hands in their pockets while at the store. This simple act, which others might regard as trivial or commonplace, can potentially be misconstrued as an intent to shoplift, leading to unjust accusations.

It is heart-wrenching to have to instill this caution in our youth, to make them hyper-aware of their actions, in ways that can rob them of the carefree innocence youth should bring. Yet, we deem it necessary, a survival tactic in a world that too often sees them not as individuals, but as stereotypes.

The necessity of such conversations underscores the magnitude of racial biases and their pervasiveness in our society. It underlines the need for continued dialogue, education, and action in challenging and changing these stereotypes.

Recently, a news article made headlines, accusing dozens of individuals of trafficking drugs for Mexican cartels. It's here that media bias subtly but powerfully plays a role in reinforcing stereotypes. The headline conveniently left out an important detail - most of the accused were white. This omission served as a catalyst for misguided assumptions about Mexican immigrants, reinforcing a damaging stereotype that they are primarily involved in drug trafficking. Such misleading headlines not only fuel racial bias but also foster a climate of fear and mistrust against a particular ethnic group.

It is, therefore, the responsibility of media entities to report objectively, ensuring their headlines and content are accurate and do not perpetuate harmful stereotypes. As consumers of news, it is equally our responsibility to critique and question the information we consume, rather than accept it at face value. In doing so, we can collectively work towards dismantling biases and building a more inclusive society.

Recognizing the presence of crime in every society, it's crucial to note that criminal behavior transcends racial, ethnic, or socioeconomic boundaries. However, the grave issue of racial profiling makes us jump to unfair and unjust conclusions too quickly. The wrongful association of certain racial or ethnic groups with crime not only perpetuates harmful stereotypes but also creates a barrier to the progression towards a more understanding and accepting society.

It's essential to realize that our words and actions, however unintended, can inflict pain and hurt on people from different races or ethnicities. A poorly chosen comment or an ill-thought-out action can alienate and marginalize individuals, heightening the divide between different racial and ethnic groups. As members of a diverse and multicultural society, we should strive for more sensitivity in our interactions, fostering mutual respect and understanding, rather than contributing to the alienation and discrimination that stem from profiling.

At times, our lack of exposure or understanding of other cultures can lead to unintended offenses.

For instance, having grown up in Ghana, I was unfamiliar with certain words or actions considered derogatory in America, and it was an eye-opening experience when I moved here. Navigating the cultural differences and learning the nuances of American societal norms and etiquette has been a journey of growth and understanding for me. It has highlighted the importance of cultural sensitivity and the need for open-mindedness in embracing and understanding different cultures. It's been a process of continuous learning, and I am still on that path.

Education is crucial in breaking down stereotypes and combating bias. Teaching about different cultures and histories can help dispel the myths and misunderstandings that contribute to discriminatory attitudes. It can also promote empathy and understanding, encouraging people to step out of their comfort zones and learn more about others' experiences.

Through my numerous conversations and interactions, I have come to understand that there is a willingness to learn in our society. Many people are eager to broaden their horizons, understand different cultural perspectives, and become more sensitive and respectful in their interactions. This desire to learn, however, can be overshadowed by a fear of making mistakes or being labeled as racist.

Understandably, nobody wants to be labeled with a term that is loaded with negative connotations and implications. This fear can lead us to become defensive about our actions or words, even when they are pointed out as potentially offensive or insensitive. But it's crucial to remember that the objective of such conversations is not to accuse or label, but to educate and foster understanding.

It's important to approach these discussions with an open mind, ready to learn and grow from them. Embrace the discomfort that may come with it, for it is through such discomfort that we truly learn and broaden our perspectives. Nobody is perfect. We're all on a continuous journey of learning and growth. It's okay to make mistakes, so long as you take those as opportunities to learn and improve. As we continue this journey, we gradually build a more inclusive and understanding society, one interaction at a time.

Instead of adhering to defensive tactics, let's choose a different path.

The first step is to *Listen.* It's crucial to pay attention, not just to respond, but to understand the perspective being presented.

This is followed by *Modifying our behavior.* If it's pointed out that certain actions or words can cause discomfort or offense, it's important to reflect, learn, and make necessary changes.

Next, is to *Be an ally.* This means standing with those who face discrimination or injustice, even if it doesn't directly affect me. It's about using our privilege to support and amplify voices that are often silenced or overlooked.

Being mindful of our actions and words is also crucial. It's necessary to be conscious of the impact of our conduct and communication, and to strive to be respectful and understanding at all times.

Speaking up and being a voice for others is another essential step. If we see discrimination or injustice, it's our responsibility to call it out, even if it's uncomfortable. It's about being brave enough to stand up for what's right, regardless of the circumstances.

Lastly, even when provoked or misunderstood, let us strive to *Hold our tongue when we have the urge to cuss and yell* (this especially applies to me). It's about maintaining respect and dignity in all engagements, and avoiding unnecessary escalation of conflict.

As we continue to walk this path, let's strive to contribute to a more empathetic and understanding society where we combat prejudice and antagonism. Each one of us bears the responsibility to challenge and change the societal structures that perpetuate racism.

We must confront our biases, educate ourselves, and elevate the voices of the marginalized. Anti-racism, however, is not a state but a constant endeavor. It requires us to critically examine our thoughts and actions every day. In this continuous journey, let us pledge to uphold the principles of respect, empathy, and understanding. Let us remember that the struggle against racism doesn't end when the noise fades away. It is a long-term commitment to creating a world where everyone is treated with dignity and respect.

It is essential to recognize and confront our own biases, and work ardently to dismantle them. Creating an inclusive society requires active participation and commitment from each one of us.

As we conclude this chapter, we invite you to reflect and ponder upon the following thoughts.

Reflections:

1. How do you plan on avoiding racist inclinations within yourself?

2. How will you contribute to fostering a sense of belonging in your community and beyond?

Xenophobia

Xenophobia

"Embrace each other by showing little acts of kindness." - Oheneyere Gifty Anti

In a heartening conversation with Ghanaian media personality, Oheneyere Gifty Anti, we broached the topic of xenophobia. Oheneyere shared insights drawn from her rich life experiences, shedding light on both the traditional Ghanaian spirit of hospitality towards foreigners, and the darker shades of xenophobia that she's encountered in her travels.

In the traditional Ghanaian culture, foreigners are treated with utmost respect and generosity, often receiving the very best the host has to offer. However, Oheneyere noted with regret that the world appears to be shifting away from such open-armed embrace.

During her 2020 book tour, she bore witness to an unfortunate incident where a Black British citizen was repeatedly questioned about his original roots, despite presenting his British passport. The time, place, and manner of questioning smacked of an undercurrent of racism and xenophobia, unnecessary and deeply disconcerting.

Yet, Oheneyere's experiences have also shown her the enormous benefits of welcoming others into one's life. Out of the 82 individuals in her Masters in Journalism class, 72 hailed from different countries, offering a vibrant tapestry of cultural perspectives and experiences. In the years since her graduation, this diverse alumni network has served as a rich resource for professional collaboration and advice.

Practicing what she preaches, Oheneyere, a Christian, regularly hosts programs for individuals of diverse denominations, religious affiliations, and cultures. In her words, "Embrace each other by showing little acts of kindness."

Through her words and actions, Oheneyere Gifty Anti practices inclusivity and tolerance, reminding us that diversity is not a threat, but a treasure to be cherished. In the face of rising xenophobia, her message serves as a timely and potent antidote, urging us to welcome, not shun the 'other'.

Commentary

The term "xenophobia" is rooted in the Greek words "Xenos," which translates to "stranger" or "foreigner," and "phobo," meaning "fear." Consequently, xenophobia can be succinctly defined as a fear of strangers or foreigners.

This explanation, however, only scratches the surface of this complex social issue.

At a deeper level, xenophobia represents an irrational or unreasoned fear, dislike or prejudice against people from other countries, cultures, or ethnic groups. It materializes in many ways, including racial slurs, discrimination, and violence against individuals perceived as foreign or different. The fear stems not just from the unfamiliarity with the 'other', but also a perceived threat to social, cultural, or national identity and security.

This fear can be amplified by socio-economic factors, political rhetoric, and media portrayals. In a rapidly globalizing world, understanding and addressing xenophobia is vital to promoting social cohesion and inclusivity. As Oheneyere Gifty Anti advocates, the antidote to xenophobia lies in embracing diversity and showing acts of kindness towards one another. By breaking down barriers and fostering understanding, we can build a more tolerant and harmonious society.

Historical cases demonstrate how even minor cultural differences or national identities can incite fear and animosity. A poignant example of this can be found in West Africa. During the late 1980s, Nigeria, a country on the verge of an economic boom, witnessed a significant influx of immigrants from neighboring Ghana. These individuals were seeking better job opportunities and a higher standard of living. Despite their shared African heritage, many Nigerians reacted negatively to this influx. Their fears were not rooted in racial or ethnic differences, but in concerns over economic stability, job competition, and social disruption. This example serves as a stark reminder that xenophobia can arise from a multitude of factors, and transcends the simplistic view of it being solely a reaction to skin color or ethnic differences.

Reflecting on the global history of xenophobia, one cannot overlook the situation in South Africa. Prior to 1994, instances of violence and antagonism against immigrants were not uncommon in this country. The end of apartheid did not immediately dissipate the deeply entrenched fears and prejudices against the 'other'. South African nationals, influenced by a myriad of social, economic, and political factors, still exhibited xenophobic attitudes.

This fear of the unfamiliar resulted in tragic instances of violence and discrimination in South Africa. Despite the shared struggle against colonialism and the common African heritage, immigrants from Zimbabwe,

Mozambique, and other neighboring countries were often met with hostility rather than solidarity. They became scapegoats for a range of societal issues, from unemployment to crime, reinforcing the cycle of xenophobia.

These examples serve to underscore the pervasive and multifaceted nature of xenophobia. It is not bound by geography, culture, or time. From Nigeria to South Africa, this irrational fear of the 'other' has manifested in varying degrees, driven by a complex interplay of factors. Understanding these nuances is key to developing effective strategies to combat xenophobia and promote a more inclusive and harmonious global society.

In situations where job opportunities are scarce and the economic climate is uncertain, immigrants are often perceived as competition, threatening the livelihood of native inhabitants.

This tension is exacerbated by existing economic disparities and the struggle for resources, intensifying the fear and resentment towards 'the other'.

Similarly, the absence of trust contributes to the perpetuation of xenophobia. In the absence of open dialogue and opportunities for intercultural interaction, these misconceptions persist, fostering an environment of fear and hostility.

Furthermore, the fear of the unknown is a fundamental human trait that can stimulate xenophobic sentiments leading to apprehension and defensiveness. Consequently, individuals may resort to isolation, discrimination, or violence as a misguided attempt to protect themselves from perceived threats.

The 2020 COVID-19 pandemic stirred up a global surge in xenophobia, a dark undercurrent to an already devastating health crisis. Fueled by fear and uncertainty, people around the world began to point fingers, assigning blame for the virus' spread. Racial bias and baseless assumptions took root, with individuals of Asian descent often unjustly perceived as potential carriers of the virus. This led to a widespread discomfort and mistrust, particularly towards those traveling from countries with high infection rates.

Shockingly, the pandemic also marked a significant increase in the marginalization of the black community in China. Faced with an unprecedented health threat, fear distorted perceptions, people of African descent became unjust targets of suspicion. In a heartbreaking display of xenophobia, many were evicted from their homes, despite having paid their rent in advance, over unfounded fears of virus transmission.

Discrimination didn't stop at housing. Certain restaurants, succumbing to the heightening xenophobia, posted signs refusing service to black customers. This blatant act of discrimination served as a stark reminder of the pervasive racial prejudices that can be inflamed in times of crisis.

The scapegoating took an even more distressing turn when black medical professionals on the frontline of combating the virus and saving lives, were singled out and blamed for the further spread of the virus. In a violation of their rights, individuals were forced into quarantine despite testing negative for the virus. This act underscored the rampant prejudice, where fear and misinformation were used to justify overt racial discrimination. The irony was stark, as those who had devoted themselves to the cause of public health were subjected to public scorn, further illuminating the deep-seated biases that were being brought to the surface in the wake of the crisis.

However, amidst the darkness and division, stories of hope and unity also emerged. People from all walks of life came together to stand in solidarity against xenophobia and discrimination. Social media campaigns were launched, calling for an end to racism and prejudice. Communities rallied around those who had been unjustly targeted, offering support and kindness in the face of hatred.

The incidents of xenophobia are prevalent in today's society, often fueled by damaging portrayals in media and political rhetoric. It is not uncommon to see immigrants depicted as criminals, a stereotype perpetuated by certain media houses and leaders. Their one-sided narratives paint immigrants as thieves, rapists, gang members, and social burdens, casting a dark shadow over their identity and contributions. This kind of representation warps public perception, leading to a deep-seated fear and suspicion of people from other countries.

As a result, some immigrants are met with hostility, xenophobia, prejudice, and discrimination, further inflaming the already tense social dynamics. The consequence of such stereotyping is a society divided by fear and misunderstanding, a community fragmented by its own bias and prejudice.

Being a foreigner in a country does not inherently mean that the person poses a threat to the people of that nation. Many foreigners bring with them talent, skill, and a genuine desire to contribute positively to their new communities.

In fact, during the COVID-19 crisis, countless frontline workers were immigrants, putting themselves at risk in countries far from their own to help combat the pandemic. They served selflessly in hospitals, care homes, and other essential services, embodying resilience and humanity in the face of unprecedented challenges. Their unwavering commitment clearly exemplified that immigrant workers are not burdens, but instead invaluable assets that enrich the societies they join. It's a narrative that urgently needs to be highlighted in our conversations, as it fosters understanding and appreciation, helping to bridge the divides that xenophobia and prejudice create.

For instance, when former Prime Minister Boris Johnson of the United Kingdom contracted the

COVID-19 virus, it was the tireless efforts of three nurses that were critical to his recovery. Two of these nurses - one from New Zealand and the other from Portugal - had been at his bedside for a critical 48 hours when his condition could have worsened significantly. They had taken on the responsibility of taking care of him, monitoring his condition, and intervening immediately if required, regardless of the potential risk to their own health. Their dedication and unwavering commitment to their duty is testament to the critical role immigrants play in the societies they join. These nurses, who came from countries far from the UK, were on the front lines, enabling the recovery of the nation's leader. Their story provides a powerful counter-narrative to the often skewed depiction of immigrants, demonstrating the invaluable contributions they make and the profound impact they have on the wellbeing of their adopted communities. It's a narrative that deserves to be told and acknowledged widely, cultivating a more inclusive, understanding, and appreciative society.

Numerous accounts further illustrate the selfless contributions of immigrant healthcare workers.

For instance, consider the story of my friend, who is a Black Muslim woman born in Ghana. She was working in an American nursing home when the pandemic hit. Despite not having access to the required Personal Protective Equipment (PPE), she did not shy away from her duties. She ingeniously improvised trash bags to protect herself, while continuing to provide care and comfort to the residents. Her actions not only demonstrated her commitment to her profession but also her deep-seated compassion. She was there, holding the hands of patients in their most vulnerable moments, offering comfort and reassurance.

This account, and others like it, tell a story that goes beyond national boundaries, ethnicity or faith. They paint a picture of humanity united in a common cause. The kindness and selflessness shown by numerous foreigners in their adopted countries affirm that there are good people everywhere. These stories serve as a powerful testimony to the positive impact and indelible contributions of immigrants, further reinforcing the need for an inclusive and appreciative discourse in our societies.

Small gestures of kindness, such as a warm smile or a kind word, hold incredible power to influence and shape perceptions. These seemingly insignificant acts can ripple outwards, promoting positive attitudes and fostering acceptance. For instance, when we greet our foreign neighbors with the same enthusiasm and warmth as we would our own kin, we're not only extending a hand of friendship but also subtly conveying the message that we value their presence and contribution.

This message is particularly important for the impressionable minds of our children. Children, by nature, are unprejudiced - they do not discern based on nationality or ethnicity. Their world is one of curiosity and openness. As they age, their perceptions begin to mirror those of the adults around them. They adopt our attitudes, our prejudices, and our biases. If we want future generations to be welcoming and inclusive, we must embody these values ourselves. We need to set an example of acceptance and kindness, to show them that every person, regardless of their origin or background, has a unique story to tell and contributions to make.

We may not always get it right, and that's okay. We're all learning, growing, and navigating through the rich tapestry of different cultures, languages, and traditions. It's paramount to remember that while there may be a few who pose challenges, the majority are simply seeking a life of peace and prosperity, much like ourselves. They bring with them unique skills, perspectives, and contributions that enrich our societies.

Let's not allow the actions of a few to tarnish our perception of the many. Instead, let's cultivate an environment of acceptance and inclusivity, one where voices are valued, and individuals are welcomed as an integral part of the community.

Remember, as we grow more globally interconnected, it becomes increasingly essential to cultivate an inclusive perspective. This journey begins with self-awareness and extends outwards to the connections we make.

As we close this chapter, I encourage you to take a moment to ponder on the following reflective questions intended to inspire introspection and incite action.

Reflections

1. Take a look at your social and professional circles. Who is in your network? Do they mirror your own background and experiences, or does your network represent a diverse range of cultures, backgrounds, and perspectives? What steps can you take to broaden your network?

2. Reflect on your interactions with people from different countries. Have you reached out to someone from a different country? What did these interactions teach you? How did they expand your understanding of the world and challenge your preconceptions?

Colorism

Colorism

"We can combat stereotypes and biases by having discussions." - Alicia D. Williams

This chapter focuses on an issue that, while pervasive, is often overlooked in our discussions on race and discrimination - colorism. At the intersection of racism and classism, colorism is a deeply ingrained societal issue that creates harmful divides and perpetuates stereotypes within communities.

But how do we initiate conversations about such a sensitive and often overlooked topic? How do we broach the subject without alienating or offending? How do we, as individuals and communities, begin to challenge our own internalized biases?

In our exploration of colorism, we turn to the experiences of Newbery and Kirkus prize award-winning author Alicia D. Williams, whose moving bestseller, Genesis Begins Again, grapples with the issue. Born into a family where her mother was light-skinned and her father's side was dark, Williams experienced colorism first-hand as she grew up.

Throughout her childhood, Williams observed how attributes like intellect, beauty, and charisma were often tied to skin color, a bias even perpetuated by elders at her church who showed favoritism towards light-skinned children. These experiences deeply informed her perspective on colorism, inspiring her to use her writing to educate the younger generation.

Living in a world where even five-year-olds tend to choose white dolls over black ones, Williams understands the urgency of addressing colorism. Through her work, she aims to inspire children to embrace their own beauty and accept their natural hair.

According to Williams, colorism is often only discussed in snippets, and she urges us not to sweep this pervasive issue under the rug. By sharing her experiences and insights, Williams is playing a crucial role in initiating the conversations that can lead to change.

Commentary

I love my Mama's beautiful black skin, rich and radiant. I remember, however, a time when I was younger, I found a sponge while playing and innocently decided that I was going to scrub her skin to make her lighter. At that tender age, nobody had explicitly told me that it was wrong to be dark-skinned. Yet, somewhere deep in my subconscious, a notion took root - the idea that if I could make Mama a little bit lighter, she'd be prettier. This memory serves as a stark reminder of the tricky nature of colorism. The biases that it instills can permeate even the most innocent minds, shaping perceptions of beauty from an early age.

During my elementary school years, there were a few kids of mixed race, who stood as enigmas in my young, curious mind. Their uniqueness was intriguing - they seemed to effortlessly straddle two distinct worlds. Their hair, softer and less coarse than mine, seemed to make them the 'cool' kids. Some of them, with their lighter skin tones, could even pass for white.

However, back then, I was oblivious to the concept of colorism. The term was foreign to me, its implications and impacts unknown. It was only in the years that followed, as I delved deeper into societal norms and prejudices, did I come to realize the unfair advantages that could come with lighter skin.

Colorism, as defined by the National Network for Civil Justice (NNCJ.org), is "a practice of discrimination by which those with lighter skin are treated more favorably than those with darker skin." This form of prejudice often goes unnoticed, operating under the radar of mainstream discourse, yet its impacts are profound and far-reaching. It extends beyond mere physical appearances and infiltrates various social domains, affecting individuals' access to opportunities, resources, and societal privileges.

Lighter skin, often associated with beauty, intelligence, and affluence, is privileged over darker skin in many societies, including the United States, the United Kingdom and India. This bias cultivates a culture of division and inferiority, perpetuating harmful stereotypes and impacting the self-esteem of those who do not fit into the societal ideal of light skin. It is a complex issue that intersects with other forms of discrimination such as racism and classism, creating a multi-layered web of bias.

Unpacking the layers of colorism requires us to critically examine the systems, norms, and beliefs that perpetuate these biases. It compels us to confront the uncomfortable truths about societal ideals of beauty, and challenge the structures that uphold these unfair standards.

Dismantling colorism is not just about changing perceptions of skin color, but about dismantling a system that privileges some while marginalizing others based on arbitrary physical characteristics.

The manifestation of colorism is pervasive and finds its way into various aspects of our lives, including media, corporate world, and personal relationships. In the realm of television and film, lighter-skinned Black individuals often secure more roles and visibility than their darker-skinned counterparts. This skewed representation not only reinforces harmful stereotypes, but also fosters a distorted worldview that marginalizes the experiences and stories of dark-skinned individuals.

Similarly, the corporate world is not immune to the effects of colorism. Studies have shown that lighter-skinned Black individuals are often perceived as more competent and are more likely to occupy positions of authority. Such prejudiced perceptions, entrenched in color bias, can result in unequal career opportunities and wage disparities, further widening the socio-economic gap.

In romantic relationships, colorism manifests through the preference for lighter-skinned partners, a bias that is frequently perpetuated by societal norms and pop culture. This preference, often subconscious, is influenced by societal ideals of beauty that privilege lighter skin tones. It can lead to decreased self-esteem among those with darker skin.

It's indeed disheartening to acknowledge that dark-skinned boys, and men, are often hastily and unjustly labeled as 'bad boys' within our societies. This harmful stereotype stems from a long-standing bias that associates darker skin tones with negative characteristics and behaviors. Consequently, these individuals face a host of challenges and barriers, particularly in the job market.

In the professional realm, specifically in the context of white-collar jobs, this stereotype can have a strong and detrimental impact. Light-skinned individuals are often favored for these positions, an implicit bias that is fueled by the incorrect and damaging assumption that they are inherently more competent, trustworthy, or suitable for such roles. This bias could contribute to a cycle of unemployment, underemployment, and socio-economic disparity. Therefore it's crucial to confront and address these prejudices within our societies and institutions.

Similarly, dark-skinned women often grapple with stereotypes that label them as loud, confrontational, and aggressive. Such damaging portrayals have their roots in historical constructs and have been perpetuated by media and culture. These prejudiced assumptions ignore the nuances of individual personalities and impose a monolithic identity onto all dark-skinned women, thereby affecting their personal, social, and professional lives.

In work environments, these stereotypes can lead to bias in hiring practices, fewer opportunities for growth, and a toxic culture that undermines their contributions and abilities. In social and interpersonal relationships, these stereotypes can result in biased perceptions and unfair treatment.

In the historical context of American slavery, a substantial bias favored lighter-skinned slaves, who were often granted privileges denied to their darker-skinned counterparts. This bias manifested itself in a multitude of ways. Lighter-skinned slaves were often assigned less physically demanding roles, such as house servants or artisans, while darker-skinned slaves were predominantly relegated to field work.

Additionally, lighter-skinned slaves were occasionally provided with educational opportunities. Slave owners, operating under misguided and racially-biased beliefs, often perceived lighter-skinned slaves as being more intellectually capable.

This historical colorism has left a lasting legacy, with its impacts still being felt today. The preferential treatment of lighter-skinned individuals has been perpetuated throughout generations, influencing societal attitudes and institutional practices that continue to privilege lighter skin tones. To challenge and overturn these deeply ingrained prejudices, it is essential that we confront the historical roots of colorism, educate ourselves and others about its harmful impacts.

Despite denials from King Charles of England regarding inquiries into the potential skin color of the Duke and Duchess of Sussex's future children, certain media outlets have maintained that a level of concern did exist within the Royal Family about the skin tone of the Sussex's offspring. These allegations, if true, serve to underscore the lasting impacts of historical colorism and how deeply it is ingrained in our society, even at the most privileged levels. This alleged incident within the Royal Family, a hereditary institution that wields significant societal influence, underscores the urgent need for continued education and dialogue surrounding racial prejudices.

The bias shown towards dark-skinned individuals is not an isolated phenomenon, but rather, it is interconnected with the broader issue of racism. This bias, insidiously operates within the same racial or ethnic group, privileging those with lighter skin over those with darker skin. This internalized racism, where a person's worth and acceptance within a community are often judged by the lightness of their skin, has its roots in colonial mentality, where whiteness was associated with purity, power, and privilege.

This correlation between skin color and societal acceptance is not only unjust but also perpetuates damaging stereotypes and discriminatory practices. It fuels a racial hierarchy that privileges lightness and penalizes darkness, creating societal imbalances and fostering animosity within communities. As such, understanding and challenging colorism is a crucial aspect of combating racism.

The rise of dark-skinned celebrities such as Viola Davis and Idris Elba to the pinnacle of global fame is a testament to a slowly but surely changing world. Davis, an Academy Award-winning actress, has repeatedly used her platform to highlight the struggles and discrimination faced by dark-skinned individuals in Hollywood. Similarly, Elba, a Golden Globe-winning actor, has broken barriers in an industry that has often typecast people of color in stereotypical roles.

Their success is not just their personal victory; it symbolizes a gradual shift in societal attitudes. Such notable progress reinforces the idea that the corrosive effects of colorism can be challenged, and the traditional norms of beauty, worth, and acceptability can be redefined.

However, it is essential to remember that these achievements, while significant, are still the exceptions rather than the norm. To truly evolve, society needs to continue challenging and deconstructing the deep-rooted biases associated with skin color.

The lingering prejudices based on skin color are a testament to the deep-seated biases that continue to mar our societal fabric. It is imperative to shift our focus away from superficial characteristics such as skin color. We ought to remind ourselves of the adage, 'don't judge a book by its cover.' The fight against colorism is a collective responsibility that demands concerted and continuous efforts.

As we conclude this discussion on colorism, let's take a moment to reflect on our personal experiences and attitudes. Remember, these questions are not about finding the 'right' answers. Instead, they are designed to stimulate thought, promote self-awareness, and encourage an open dialogue.

Reflections

1. Have you ever experienced or witnessed colorism in your own life? If so, how did you react? What emotions did this evoke in you?

2. Have you ever found yourself making assumptions about others based on their skin color? How might these assumptions have influenced your interactions with them?

3. Are there facets of your identity that you feel have been overshadowed by the color of your skin?

Yellow Peril and Asian Hate

Yellow Peril and Asian Hate

"One of the keys to stopping hate is to start seeing people as humans." - Dr. Esther Godfrey

Dr. Esther Godfrey, an English professor at the University of South Carolina (USC) Upstate, grew up with a unique vantage point on Asian-American experiences, her mother being a Chinese immigrant. Her research work, spanning both literature and issues on gender and race, provides a profound understanding of the complexities surrounding these subjects. This understanding is especially poignant in light of violence against Asian Americans, a behavior that has left many of us asking: Why would anyone want to attack people?

According to Dr. Godfrey, the origins of this violence can be traced back to harmful propaganda rooted in fear and ignorance, which she connects to the historic concept of

'Yellow Peril'. The term, born out of an era of imperialism, was used to spread fear and racist beliefs about Chinese, Korean, and Japanese people. It painted them as dangerous and thus, justified their subjugation.

To Dr. Godfrey, the key to combating this hate lies in our voices. We often remain shockingly silent in moments of overt racism, either out of surprise or uncertainty on how to react. But as Dr. Godfrey suggests: it's crucial to correct people when they make harmful remarks or stereotypes, document instances of racism, and report any racist incidents. Safety should always be the priority for the person being attacked.

Our responsibilities extend beyond immediate reactions to such incidents.

It's equally important to check in with our Asian or Pacific Islander peers. If you're not acquainted with someone who's Asian, reach out. The world has never been more connected, and numerous AAPI organizations are just a click away, offering a wealth of knowledge about the diverse cultures within the Asian community.

As we strive to stop the hate, we must remember that this starts with seeing each other as humans, not racially defined entities. We can learn from history, stand up for our peers, and above all, foster an environment of respect and understanding. Together, we can dismantle the chains of fear and prejudice.

Commentary

Through Dr. Godfrey's words, we are reminded of the fundamental need for humanizing each other. Together, let's reflect on the importance of perceiving each individual beyond their ethnic origins or skin color, instead acknowledging the shared humanity that binds us.

The COVID-19 pandemic, originating from Wuhan, China, inadvertently unleashed a wave of fear and xenophobia towards Asians worldwide. This misinformation led to a disturbing increase in hate crimes, impacting the Asian community significantly. The derogatory misnomer, "Chinese Virus," became a catalyst, further inflating the misguided suspicion and outright hostility towards this community. This label not only oversimplified the pandemic's origin but also generalized an extremely diverse group – stigmatizing and discriminating against them based on a health crisis beyond anyone's control.

This rise in hate crimes is not an isolated event but an alarming manifestation of deeply-seated prejudices that need to be addressed on a societal level. Hence it is essential to debunk the harmful stereotypes, counteract the spread of misinformation and foster an environment of mutual respect and understanding.

However, we must understand that the wave of xenophobia was not only targeted towards the Chinese. Considered a monolithic group by the uninformed, Asians from diverse backgrounds bore the brunt of these hate crimes. Native Hawaiians and Pacific Islanders, often overlooked in conversations about the Asian community, reported a surge in incidents of racial harassment and violence. People originating from Hong Kong, Korea, and Vietnam, despite having distinct cultures and no direct connection to the pandemic's origin, also found themselves the targets of misplaced hostility. Moreover, individuals from other Asian countries, including but not limited to Japan, the Philippines, and India, faced similar prejudices. The xenophobia indiscriminately impacted everyone seen to be of Asian descent, underscoring the need to recognize and respect the diversity that exists within the Asian community and highlighting the urgency to combat widespread misinformation and prejudice.

This highlights a lack of cultural awareness and understanding that fuels generalizations and stereotypes. It's not uncommon to find instances where individuals from Korea, Japan, Vietnam, or other Asian countries are mistakenly referred to as Chinese by those unfamiliar with the diversity within the Asian continent. This ignorance might stem from a lack of exposure to or education about the rich and varied cultures, languages, and histories that exist within Asia.

Each Asian country has its own unique heritage, traditions, and socio-political context that shape its people's identities and experiences. Misidentifying an individual's cultural background not only dismisses these nuances but also contributes to the harmful monolithization of Asians. This simplification can lead to skewed perceptions and misguided reactions, as witnessed during the rise in hate crimes during the pandemic. Combatting this issue requires greater emphasis on cultural education.

These anecdotal instances vividly illustrate the stigmatization and social isolation experienced by many Asians during the height of the pandemic. In some communities, false beliefs about the virus' origin and transmission led to baseless fear and avoidance of people of Asian descent. For example, there were accounts of Asian children being ostracized in their own neighborhoods, unable to ride their bikes or play outdoors due to unfounded concerns that they might spread the virus.

Further away from Asia, in African countries like Ghana, the repercussions of pandemic-induced xenophobia was brewing. In one notable incident, an Asian man who had been residing there was singled out and avoided in public. Despite being a part of the local community, he found himself alone on a minibus, with fellow passengers refusing to sit near him due to misplaced fears of contagion.

Even before the advent of COVID-19, there has been a deeply ingrained history of scapegoating, bigotry, and hostility against

Asians. This bias often flares during periods of war, economic unrest, and even in seemingly innocuous settings like schools and workplaces.

For instance, during the Second World War, Japanese-Americans were unfairly interned due to irrational fears and prejudice. Similarly, during periods of economic downturn, Asians, especially those from the Southeast and Pacific regions, have often been unfairly targeted as they are stereotypically viewed as "stealing jobs" from locals.

In academic settings, the 'model minority' myth frequently associated with Asians can be double-edged. While it might seem like a positive stereotype, it can create immense pressure on individuals to conform to high academic standards, leading to undue stress and mental health issues. It also feeds into the harmful narrative that all Asians are the same - academically inclined, hardworking, and successful, thereby overlooking the diverse individual experiences and struggles within these communities.

Workplace discrimination has also been a pressing issue for Asians and Pacific Islanders. Many face the 'bamboo ceiling,' a term referring to the obstacles that prevent Asian professionals from moving up the corporate ladder, irrespective of their qualifications or achievements. Stereotypes that Asians are passive or lack leadership qualities often contribute to this bias, furthering inequality and impeding career progression.

These long-standing stereotypes and biases against Asians are not novel phenomena born out of the pandemic. They have merely been amplified and made more visible in the wake of the COVID-19 crisis, underscoring the urgent necessity for systemic change and increased cultural understanding.

The pervasive myth that all Asians excel academically, particularly in STEM fields, masks a harsh reality: not all Asians are affluent or successful, and many are living below the poverty line. While it's true that a significant number of Asians occupy roles in high-paying tech and engineering fields, this single narrative often overshadows the diversity within the Asian population. The stereotype that all Asians are successful, wealthy, and educated can lead to the dismissal of the very real struggles experienced by Asian communities, particularly those who suffer from higher poverty rates. It's crucial to challenge this monolithic portrayal and acknowledge the socio-economic disparities within Asian communities to ensure that those in need are not overlooked.

By breaking down these stereotypes, society can work towards providing necessary support and resources to all Asians, not just those who fit into the successful 'model minority' narrative.

The familiar tune of "Jesus Loves the Little Children" by Cedarmont Kids carries a powerful and timely message, particularly in light of the discussed stereotypes and biases.

Here it goes:
Jesus loves the little children
All the children of the world
Red and yellow, black and white
They are precious in His sight

Jesus loves the little children of the world

The simple lyrics of this song encapsulate a profound truth: regardless of racial or ethnic background, every individual is valuable and loved. The song emphasizes the concept of universal love and acceptance by using colors - red, yellow, black, and white - as metaphors for the diverse range of human races and cultures. The lyrics serve as a reminder that, in the eyes of divine love, there is no room for discrimination or bias.

Moreover, the song presents a challenge to humans to emulate this form of universal, unprejudiced love. It's an invitation to reject stereotypes and biases, and instead, to view every individual as worthy and 'precious in His sight.' In this context, the song serves as a counter-narrative against the harmful stereotypes plaguing Asian communities and other minority groups. It encourages listeners to reject the idea of a 'model minority' or the notion that a person's worth or success can be determined by their ethnicity. Instead, it promotes the understanding that all people, irrespective of their socio-economic status or cultural heritage, are equally significant and deserving of respect, love, and opportunities.

As we conclude this chapter, it's essential to reflect on our personal experiences and interactions with various cultures and races. These reflections can help us recognize our own biases, acknowledge the rich diversity of human experiences. We each have a role to play in challenging stereotypes and supporting diversity; the journey begins with understanding and acknowledgement.

For example, films can offer us a glimpse into the lives, traditions, and challenges of people from diverse backgrounds, enabling us to gain a deeper understanding and appreciation of their experiences. Also, by consciously choosing to support businesses owned by people of different races, we contribute to the economic sustainability and growth of diverse communities. This small act can have a significant impact in dismantling systemic racial economic disparities.

Reflections

1. Take a moment to think: Have you ever watched a movie that explored a distinct culture different from your own?

2. Consider also your patronage of businesses. Have you ever knowingly supported a business owned by a person from a different race?

Celebrating Hispanic and Latina/o Heritage

Celebrating Hispanic and Latina/o Heritage

"When we learn about other cultures, we realize that we are more the same than different." - Dr. Begona Caballero-Garcia

Dr. Caballero-Garcia's statement rings true on so many levels. The more we immerse ourselves in different cultures, the more we uncover shared values and common grounds, which transcend the superficial differences. It's in the joy of a family dinner, the grief in a personal loss, the exuberance of festivals, or the quiet satisfaction of a hard day's work. These shared human experiences bind us all, regardless of our cultural backgrounds. It's a profound realization that underneath the diversity of traditions, languages, and customs, we are united by the same human spirit.

For the purposes of this chapter we will be using the words Hispanic, Latinos, and, Latina/o (Latinx) interchangeably.

I had the honor of hosting three remarkable Hispanic-American women on Humanity Chats. They represented Peru, Mexico, and Spain - Gia Quinones, Dr. Araceli Hernandez-Laroche, and Dr. Begona Caballero-Garcia. These dynamic women shared the richness and diversity of Hispanic Latino culture, their personal journeys, and the challenges they face in America.

Gia Quinones, a passionate advocate for mental health and suicide awareness, shared her immersion in American culture after immigrating from Peru at the age of eleven. However, she has always been keen on preserving her heritage, highlighting the significance of Hispanic Heritage Month celebrations in fostering inclusivity and honoring heritage. She further emphasized the importance of embracing diversity and understanding one's own cultural identity in creating a more welcoming society.

Dr. Araceli Hernandez-Laroche, a university professor from Mexico, expressed her desire for American schools to provide more comprehensive education about U.S. history and its neighbors. She underscored the importance of language appreciation in enhancing understanding and overcoming barriers, particularly evident during the COVID-19 crisis in the Hispanic/Latino community. Dr. Hernandez-Laroche also highlighted the need to address misconceptions and stereotypes about Hispanic/Latino individuals and their cultures.

Lastly, Dr. Begona Caballero-Garcia, an immigrant from Spain and Professor at Wofford College, shared her passion for social justice. Drawing from author Chimamanda Adichie's TED Talk, The Danger of a Single Story, where Adichie warned that "if we heard a single story about a person or country, we risk a critical understanding". - (Adichie, 2009). In the talk, Adichie shared that when she was young, she wrote about snow and ginger beer because those were the kind of stories that she had read in books. However, things changed when the author discovered African books. She started to write about the things that she recognized.

Dr. Caballero-Garcia warned against the danger of a single narrative and encouraged us to learn about the diversity within the Hispanic/Latino community. She also stressed the importance of recognizing intersectionality and how different aspects of one's identity intersect to shape an individual's experiences.

According to Quinones, Dr. Hernandez-Laroche, and Dr. Caballero-Garcia, to support and learn more about the Hispanic/Latino community, consider these action points:

- *Educate yourself about Hispanic/Latino history and honor trailblazers.*
  - *For example, the first woman who went into space was a Latina woman - Ellen Ochoa.*
  - *Celebrate trailblazers such as Justice Sonia Sotomayor*
- *Participate in cultural activities to understand the traditions, music, and cuisine.*
- *Advocate for human rights and dignity for all.*

- *Register to vote to ensure your voice is heard.*
- *Stand up against racism and be a mentor to others.*

These powerful women serve as a reminder that Hispanic Heritage Month is not just a celebration of culture, but also an opportunity to amplify the voices and stories of the Hispanic/Latino community.

By learning about other cultures, we not only celebrate diversity but also discover our shared humanity.

Commentary

The terms 'Hispanic' and 'Latino' are often used interchangeably, but as the Oxford dictionary suggests, they each have distinct definitions. 'Hispanic' denotes a connection with Spain or Spanish-speaking countries, which not only includes nations in Latin America but also encompasses Spain itself. On the other hand, 'Latino' refers specifically to individuals of Latin American origin or descent, which includes countries in Central and South America and the Caribbean. The cultures within these groups are as diverse and varied as the countries themselves, each with its own rich history, traditions, and customs. Understanding these distinctions is essential to appreciate the rich tapestry of experiences, stories, and identities within the Hispanic and Latino communities.

Additionally, it's important to recognize that there are people who identify as Afro-Latino, Indigenous Latino, or mixed heritage that may not fit neatly into specific categories.

In the many discussions and discourses about race, there's a common and oversimplified view that tends to treat Hispanics and Latinos as a homogenous culture. The truth is far from this. While these communities share common threads in language, history, and some aspects of culture, they are an incredibly diverse group. They hail from numerous countries, each with its own distinct traditions, dialects, culinary habits, and social norms.

A Mexican's experience and cultural identity, for example, may significantly differ from that of a Colombian, a Puerto Rican, or an Argentine. Recognizing and acknowledging this diversity is crucial to understanding and appreciating the nuanced experiences of Hispanics and Latinos. It allows for a more inclusive dialogue, where individual experiences can be voiced and heard, rather than being overshadowed by a broader, generalized identity.

Currently the largest minority group in the United States, Hispanics and Latinos have made indelible contributions to the fabric of American life, as well as the lives in their home countries. They have become important figures in business, politics, sports, literature, art, and science, leaving their mark in every field and industry. From creating tech startups in Silicon Valley to leading grassroots organizations in rural communities, their achievements attest to their determination, resilience, and the profound impact they've had on society.

Not only have they enriched society with their contributions, but they've also imbued it with the vibrancy of their cultural traditions and values. Moreover, their narratives of migration, assimilation, and identity formation offer valuable insights into the human condition, challenging us to reevaluate our preconceptions and assumptions about race and ethnicity.

Although we may have racial or cultural differences, learning about their culture is as important as it is valuable for them to learn about ours. This mutual exchange of cultural knowledge fosters understanding, respect, and empathy. It dilutes barriers, encourages dialogue, and promotes unity in diversity.

When we take the initiative to learn about another's culture, we not only gain knowledge about their traditions and values but also a deeper understanding of their experiences, perspectives, and worldviews. Thus, we move a step closer to eradicating stereotypes and biases, and building an inclusive society.

The power of cultural exchange is often most tangibly felt through experiences like sharing a meal, or getting lost in the pages of a book. For instance, one might savor a plate of flavorful enchiladas. Similarly, reading a book penned by a Hispanic or Latina/o author can offer an intimate glimpse into their experiences, worldviews, and expressions. Through such shared experiences, we can foster a deeper appreciation for the Hispanic and Latina/o community, bridging gaps of understanding and strengthening the fabric of our multicultural society.

Reflections

1. What is your favorite Hispanic or Latina/o meal?

2. Have you read a book written by a Hispanic or Latina/o author?

Broadening Our Lens

Broadening Our Lens

"We cannot move forward without forgiveness, positive effort, and love."

- Michel Stone

Stone's poignant remark encapsulates the essence of being open to learning about other cultures and traditions. By broadening our lens, we cultivate an environment built on the foundation of understanding and harmony.

During the volatile summer of 2020, I had the privilege of engaging in a profound conversation with Michel Stone, an award-winning author known for her insightful thoughts and compelling narratives. This interaction took place amidst the backdrop of racial tension and nationwide protests sparked by the tragic death of Mr. George Floyd. As COVID-19 disproportionately tormented minorities, leading to an alarming rise in death rates, loss of employment, and even looting in some cities, it felt as though our world was on the brink of implosion.

Michel, like many of us, initially grappled with the fear of speaking up. What if her words unintentionally caused pain, or what if her sentiments were misconstrued? Yet, after much reflection, she chose action over silence, reminding us that the first step towards change is often the most significant.

She pondered - what could happen if we started dialogues within our communities, with people we encounter in our daily routines, such as school, church, or even while shopping at the local grocery store? These interactions, no matter how seemingly small, could lead to us learning more about our fellow humans; broadening our lens.

This isn't to say that the task is easy. As Michel astutely quoted Mother Teresa, "If I look at the mass, I will never act - If I look at the one, I will." The global issues we face can feel insurmountable, leaving us feeling powerless to initiate a conversation. But it is precisely these moments when it's crucial to unite and embark on discussions that push us beyond our comfort zones.

Michel pinpointed one of the most pressing societal crises we face: confirmation bias. All too often, we sequester ourselves within echo chambers, filling our lives with voices that mirror our own views and sentiments. It is challenging, yet vital, to engage in an open, honest discourse with someone who may lead a distinctly different life.

We explored ways to see the world through our neighbor's eyes, such as active listening, diversifying our literature, embracing discomfort, and seeking commonality. Michel remembered a recent conversation that she had shared with former Converse College President - Betsy Fleming. The two women discussed the words of the American Pledge of Allegiance.

"I pledge allegiance to the flag of the United States of America, and to the republic for which it stands, one nation under God, indivisible, with liberty and justice for all."

We pondered the familiar words of the Pledge of Allegiance, especially the words "liberty and justice for all," and how this should inform our worldview. There is no qualifier - there is no liberty for these and justice for those.

If we were to take the words 'liberty and justice for all' seriously, that should dictate the lens through which we see the world.

Michel and I found consensus in the universal truth that, despite our diverse experiences and backgrounds, we share more commonalities than differences. Furthermore, we acknowledged the pain experienced by communities affected by racial disparities, proposing the practice of 'Ubuntu,' an African philosophy that translates to 'I am because of who we all are.'

In the wise words of the late Nobel Peace Prize-winning Bishop Desmond Tutu, "There is no Future Without Forgiveness." Are we prepared to forgive, listen, and learn? If we are, we can create ripples of change that broaden our collective lens and shape a more inclusive, understanding world.

Commentary

The Jollof rice debate between Ghanaians and Nigerians is a fascinating example of how our biases, especially those ingrained in us through our community and experiences, can shape our perceptions. I must admit, for the longest time, I was a staunch supporter of Ghanaian Jollof rice, convinced of its supremacy over the Nigerian version without even having tasted the latter. This belief was primarily fueled by the echoing sentiment of my community, a classic instance of confirmation bias.

After relocating to America, I ventured out of my comfort zone and tasted the much-debated Nigerian Jollof. The Nigerian Jollof was quite good. This experience taught me that it's important to question our biases and step outside our echo chambers. It's vital to experience things first-hand before forming an opinion, especially on topics that are subjective and deeply rooted in cultural pride.

This is a principle we can extend to more profound discussions around race and culture. It's a reminder that our understanding is often limited by our experiences and can be deepened through genuine exploration. Much like the different Jollof rice, each culture offers a unique flavor to the human experience, and none is inherently superior to the other.

Intrigued by the tasty Nigerian Jollof rice, I decided to further immerse myself in additional Nigerian cuisine. This exploration led me to discover other dishes such as puff-puff, 3ba, chin chin, and iyan. Each dish offered a distinctive blend of flavors that was delightful in its own right. But as I savored these Nigerian meals, I experienced a sense of déjà vu. These dishes, albeit under different names, were also staples in Ghanaian cuisine. Puff-puff was our bofrot, 3ba was our gari made with hot water, chin chin was our sugar chips, and iyan (pounded yam) mirrored our fufu.

This culinary journey served as a striking metaphor for our shared human experience. Despite our distinct ethnic backgrounds and cultures, there are numerous parallels that tie us together. Just as the names of these dishes change across borders, the experiences of people vary across races. Yet, at the core, we share common elements - a collective human heritage. This realization fosters a deeper appreciation for diversity, not as a divider, but as a thread that weaves us all together.

If I hadn't given myself the opportunity to try the different dishes, I probably wouldn't have known about the similarity in taste. You see, it's easy to stay confined within the walls of what we know, what we're comfortable with.

It's human nature to stick to the familiar. But when we allow ourselves to step outside of our comfort zone, we uncover an entire realm of experiences just waiting to be discovered.

Now let me backtrack - Although the Nigerian Jollof was good, as a true Ghanaian at heart, I'll confess, my vote still goes for Ghana Jollof. Perhaps it's a taste of home, a sense of familiarity, that gives it an upper hand.

But that's the beauty of diversity - while we can appreciate, respect, and enjoy different cultures, we also celebrate our roots, our individuality, the uniqueness of our own culture. After all, it's this incredible mix of shared experiences and unique differences that create the beautiful mosaic of humanity.

Stepping outside my culinary comfort zone to try these new dishes served as a metaphor for broader experiences in life. Just as I had to venture beyond my familiar tastes to discover the delights of Nigerian Jollof, we often need to push beyond the boundaries of our own understanding to truly appreciate the complex nuances of different races and cultures.

This process may initially seem daunting or uncomfortable, but the rewards are immeasurable. Like savoring a new dish, we enrich our minds with new perspectives, broadening our worldview and deepening our understanding of the intricate interplay of cultures. In the same way that I discovered a shared taste across different cuisines, we may also unearth shared values, beliefs, and experiences that transcend racial and cultural divides when we dare to venture beyond the confines of our own experiences. So, the lesson from this simple example is that venturing outside of our comfort zones allows us to grow, learn, and appreciate the beautiful diversity that life offers.

As basic as the example sounds, it applies to different facets of our lives. The same way that sampling different cuisines has broadened my culinary palate, learning about different cultures, religions, and political ideologies will be instrumental in shaping our perspective.

Much like the variety of ingredients in a pot of Jollof, our varying perspectives, shaped by our unique experiences and backgrounds, contribute to the beautiful, complex medley that is humanity.

There might be aspects of one's perspective that irritate you, or you might find yourself disappointed by one's personal views on world affairs. That's okay. Our differences in opinion are not a chasm, but a bridge—an opportunity for dialogue, learning, and growth.

Just as I would invite you to share a meal of Ghana Jollof, I invite you to share in a conversation, to challenge my viewpoints, and to enrich my understanding with your experiences.

The key lies in being open to learning and listening, to continually expanding our horizons. Every conversation, every shared experience, broadens the lens through which we view life, adding another layer to our understanding.

It's often said that the key to understanding is empathy, and there is no better way to foster empathy than by engaging in open and honest dialogue. By engaging with and learning from those different from us, we can only enrich our own understanding and become more compassionate, well-rounded individuals.

In conclusion, it's worth taking the time to reflect on the questions at the end of this chapter. These are not rhetorical questions, but an invitation to expand your world, one conversation at a time. Interactions can be incredibly enlightening, dismantling preconceived notions and building bridges of understanding.

Reflections

1. Are you willing to learn from someone outside your usual circle of friends? An individual whose experiences and perspective might be entirely different from yours?

2. Have you recently reached out to someone of a different race? Have you taken the opportunity to learn about their experiences, their traditions, their joys, and their struggles?

Racial Inequality

Racial Inequality

"In order for one to succeed, it's important to have an equal playing field." - Hope Blackley

We live in a world where the color of one's skin can still determine their experiences and opportunities. From education to job prospects and even life expectancy – the playing field is far from level. It's a sobering reality we must face head-on if we are to make any progress.

However, acknowledging this inequality is only the first step. It's in understanding the individual stories, the personal struggles, and triumphs, where we truly begin to see the bigger picture.

Blackley sets a compelling tone for this chapter. Her insights into racial inequalities were enlightening. She emphasized our collective responsibility to educate ourselves and others that not everyone starts life with an equal footing. Some are born into privilege while others have to work relentlessly to rise against the odds.

Education and Racial Inequality

The discussion shed light on how systemic racial inequalities seep into education, creating a chasm between potential and achievement. Blackley illustrated this point by highlighting the detrimental effects of redlining and Jim Crow laws on certain communities, linking a child's zip code to the quality of their education. Schools in disadvantaged districts often lack resources, and the home environment may not be conducive to learning.

Imagine young children, she said, left to fend for themselves due to parents working late shifts, struggling to finish homework amidst empty cupboards. This isn't just an abstract notion; it's the harsh reality for many children, and it starkly illustrates the playing field that is far from level.

Healthcare Disparities

Our conversation moved onto the healthcare sector, another realm heavily impacted by racial inequalities. It was not just the uninsured status of patients; other factors such as language barriers and lack of access to healthy foods, education, and amenities significantly affected these communities' health outcomes. Despite the strides made in healthcare, Black and Latino communities continue to bear a disproportionate burden of health disparities. These disparities range from higher rates of chronic diseases such as diabetes and hypertension to higher mortality rates from diseases like cancer. Many Black and Latino individuals face hurdles in accessing quality healthcare, which are often exacerbated by language barriers, cultural differences, and systemic biases within the healthcare system. For instance, Black women are three to four times more likely to experience a pregnancy-related death than white women, and Latino communities often report higher levels of stress due to discrimination, which can lead to mental health problems. (I hope these statistics have improved since the publishing of this book).

While racial and ethnic disparities in healthcare are deeply rooted and complex to address, acknowledging their existence and understanding their causes is the first step towards creating equitable health systems. It is critical to approach healthcare reform not just from a policy perspective, but also from a social determinants standpoint—addressing economic stability, education, social and community context, health and healthcare, and neighborhood and built environment.

Achieving health equity requires a multifaceted approach that dismantles systemic barriers and builds a healthcare system that serves everyone with the dignity and care they deserve.

Economic Empowerment

Touching upon economic empowerment, Blackley shared the harsh reality of being equally or more qualified yet overlooked for advancement due to race. She proposed a radical idea – what if the top one percent considered sacrificing an extra home or luxury vehicle? Perhaps, she suggested, we could find ways to uplift those who need it most.

Blackley's concluding thoughts were a call to unity. She urged us to stop blaming individuals for not knowing better and instead, work together towards a solution. This journey, she asserted, must be led by our white brothers and sisters for our society to truly advance.

Blackley's candid conversation is a stark reminder of the work that needs to be done. Yet, it reminds us about the possibilities and available opportunities.

As our conversation came to an end, Blackley left us with an important message - change starts with each one of us. Whether it is educating ourselves about systemic inequalities, actively supporting organizations working towards racial justice, or simply having open and honest conversations about race, we all have a role to play in creating a more equitable society.

Commentary

Understanding both the positive and negative aspects of society is crucial for affecting change. It is through this understanding that we can appreciate the progress we've made, while also recognizing the areas where we need to improve. Knowledge is the key to understanding, and understanding is the first step towards change.

During one of our Humanity Chats, **Sumi Mukherjee**, an Indian American hailing from Minnesota, recounted an unforgettable episode from his teenage years. His closest ally during those formative years was a white teenager who, despite their shared experiences, was incapable of perceiving the racial discrimination and bullying that Sumi routinely endured.

This narrative perfectly encapsulates the paradox that often exists in our society - the inability, or perhaps unwillingness, of certain individuals to acknowledge the presence of racial inequalities. These individuals, much like Sumi's friend, are often ensconced in their own experiences, unable to comprehend the difficulties that others may be encountering.

This isn't a story unique to Sumi or his friend. Only through recognizing and understanding these disparities can we begin to dismantle the systems that uphold them.

According to the United States Treasury Department, Racial Inequality is defined as "the unequal distribution of resources, power, and economic opportunity across race in a society." This definition lifts the veil on the reality that underpins societies globally - the uneven allocation of resources. It's not a phenomenon isolated to one country or continent, it's a global occurrence. However, the nature and degree of these inequalities can significantly vary based on location, culture, history, and several other factors.

For instance, in one society, the disparity might be primarily in the realm of educational opportunities, where the quality and access to education are heavily influenced by racial and ethnic backgrounds. In another society, it may manifest in the form of wealth gaps, with the racial divide clearly visible in the distribution of real estate, income, and other assets.

These disparities draw a vivid picture of the systemic nature of inequality, which is often deeply rooted in the historic and socio-cultural fabric of societies. It is this awareness, coupled with the willingness to engage in hard but necessary conversations that can lead us to devise more effective strategies to tackle these deeply entrenched disparities.

For example, let's take a look at the historical context in Ghana. Historically, the people from the southern part of Ghana had access to certain resources that were unavailable to the residents in the northern sector of the country. The southern regions, blessed with rich soils and favorable climatic conditions, thrived with agriculture, enabling the inhabitants to establish profitable cocoa farms. The income derived from these farms translated into better infrastructure, education, and healthcare facilities.

In contrast, the northern regions grappled with harsher climatic conditions and less fertile soils, which significantly impeded agricultural activities. With limited avenues for income, the north lagged in developmental parameters, reflecting a clear divide. Even though the people in the north worked as hard, if not harder, they couldn't match the wealth accumulation witnessed in the south.

This example illustrates how geographic location, intertwined with the race/tribe of the inhabitants, could directly influence the access to resources. While the people of the south and north shared the same national identity, the access to resources and opportunities diverged based on regional and tribal lines.

By acknowledging these historical realities, we can deepen our understanding of inequalities, and bolster our efforts towards creating strategies that address these disparities head-on.

It reminds us that the battle against racial inequality is not a one-size-fits-all approach, but requires a nuanced understanding of the unique contexts and historical factors that give rise to these disparities. This understanding paves the way for policies and initiatives that are rooted in empathy and inclusivity.

The narrative of American history, like any other, is marked by its unique geography, demographics, and socio-economic landscape. Certain areas, characterized by their prosperous zip codes, bear testimony to this uniqueness. These neighborhoods, often reflective of a higher distribution of wealth, tend to offer their inhabitants access to quality schools, diverse grocery stores, state-of-the-art hospitals, and superior amenities; all of which contribute to an enhanced standard of living and greater prospects for personal and professional growth.

In contrast, there are regions where the zip codes tell a different story. These areas, often grappling with historical disadvantages, lack access to not just economic opportunities but also basic resources. The residents find themselves embroiled in a cycle of poverty and inequality, their circumstances perpetuated by deep-seated stereotypes and a dearth of support mechanisms. This disparity is not a result of a lack of effort or ambition on the part of those inhabitants. Instead, it's a consequence of systemic disparities that have been embedded in society over the course of history.

By understanding and acknowledging these unique American realities, we can better comprehend the extent and complexity of racial and economic inequalities. It emphasizes that the resolution to these deeply rooted issues does not lie in broad, generic measures but in policies and initiatives that recognize and address these distinct historical and socio-economic contexts.

In conclusion, it's important to ask ourselves some reflection questions that will help us take proactive steps towards addressing these systemic disparities. By considering these reflection questions seriously, we can all play a part in fostering a society marked by inclusivity and equal opportunities.

This is an opportunity for us to directly contribute to breaking the cycle of inequality and paving the way for more diverse representation in various professional fields. This can be an incredibly powerful way of empowering individuals, providing them with tools to succeed and opening doors to opportunities they might not have access to otherwise. Learning from others, particularly those with different life experiences and perspectives, can greatly enhance our understanding of the world and empathy towards others. This way, we can contribute to creating an environment where every individual, regardless of their zip code/region, can reach their full potential.

Reflections

1. Will you recommend a qualified person for a job or position, regardless of their racial or economic background?

2. Are you willing to mentor someone or teach them a skill?

3. Conversely, are you open to being a mentee?

Creating Racially Equitable Systems

Creating Racially Equitable Systems

"Seek to treat others the way you want to be treated." - Ryan Langley

In a conversation on racial equity with Ryan Langley, a trial attorney from South Carolina, whose experiences range from working with the Bush administration to the Cato Institute, Langley's unique perspective, drawn from his diverse background and encapsulated in the assertion that "we all bleed the same color," serves as a potent reminder of our shared humanity.

Langley's vision of racial equity is grounded in empathy and understanding. He persuades us to step out of our comfort zones, to strive to comprehend the experiences of those who walk in different shoes.

Reflecting on a racial equity training he attended in Durham, North Carolina, he acknowledged the discomfort that can come with recognizing privilege as a white male. Yet, he insists that understanding is essential if we are to uphold the belief that all men are created equal.

Digging deeper into the systemic barriers that perpetuate racial inequity, Langley pointed to interconnected issues of race, socio-economic status, and the justice system. Drawing on the Equal Employment Opportunity Commission data, he highlighted the vicious cycle in which people of color find themselves disproportionately incarcerated, arrested, and convicted.

The cycle, Langley notes, often begins with economic disadvantage, leading individuals to accept plea deals and consequently, thrusting them into a perpetual cycle of incarceration and recidivism. Acknowledging the past is a crucial part of addressing systemic racism.

Langley reminded us of the restrictive covenants that, until relatively recently, barred black individuals from owning certain properties. The legacy of centuries of systemic advantages for white individuals, contrasted with a few decades of affirmative action, suggests a race that started long before all participants were allowed to run.

However, Langley doesn't believe in seeking a magic bullet. Instead, he proposes a multi-pronged approach to establishing racially equitable systems: give everyone a seat at the table, elevate underrepresented voices within professional spaces, get comfortable asking uncomfortable questions, and establish citizen committees to oversee the justice system. He concedes that meaningful change takes time and requires a willingness to both listen and act.

In our collective pursuit of racial equity, Langley's insights serve as a powerful reminder. We need to continuously strive towards understanding, acknowledge the past, commit to action, and, most importantly, retain our faith in the power of slow, meaningful change. This, then, is our collective call to action: let's make racial equity a reality, not just an aspiration.

Commentary

Langley's conversation reminds us to see and value each other not just as fellow human beings, but as mirrors of what we ourselves deserve: respect, fairness, and dignity.

When we say racial equity is about eliminating racial disparities and improving outcomes, we're talking about fairness. And fairness isn't just about providing equal opportunity. It requires us to acknowledge that different races have different needs and resources due to historic and systemic disparities. This understanding is at the core of a racially equitable system.

Let's consider an everyday example. Imagine a race where the starting line is systematically placed further back for some participants based on their race. Though the finish line is the same for all, the race is inherently unfair. In this context, fairness doesn't merely imply making the race open to every participant. It means adjusting the starting line so all runners are on an equal footing at the race's onset.

The same principle applies when we address systemic racism. A fair system doesn't merely offer the same opportunities to everyone. It takes into account the uneven starting lines and works to level the playing field, considering each group's unique challenges and needs. In essence, it provides different resources where necessary to ensure that everyone has the same opportunity to succeed. It's a monumental task, but as we've seen from Langley's insights, it's not insurmountable. It will require us to continually engage in difficult dialogue, listen, act, and believe in the power of slow, purposeful change.

Let's remember, racial equity isn't just about the end goal. It's about the journey towards that goal, the process of leveling the playing field, and creating a society where every individual, no matter their race, can thrive.

In conclusion, achieving racial equity is not just the task of those who have been marginalized. It's a responsibility that we all share, a journey that we all must embark on together. Only by doing so can we hope to create a society in which everyone has the equal opportunity to thrive.

I invite you to reflect on this crucial question:

Reflection:

1. Are you willing to be open-minded during discussions about equity in society?

Education

Education

"Education is the passport to the future, for tomorrow belongs to those who prepare for it today." – Malcolm X

This potent quote encapsulates the power and promise of education. It's an empowering tool that can level playing fields, break down barriers, and illuminate paths towards a brighter, more equitable tomorrow. It is through education that we can prepare the future generation – equipping them with the knowledge, understanding, and empathy to champion racial equity and reshape our society.

Education is a powerful tool, capable of sparking significant social change. Several Humanity Chats guests have underscored the impact of the educational system on life outcomes. Their insights have led us to the understanding that a myriad of strategies can be employed to positively influence the success of our communities.

Through Dr. Walter Lee of University of South Carolina - Upstate, we learned about the importance of equipping teachers with training and resources, as exemplified by the innovative Call Me MISTER program (Mentors Instructing Students Toward Effective Role Models). This program, initially launched at three Universities with Clemson serving as the headquarters, has been heralded nationally for its unique approach to addressing the challenges of our time. It aims to enhance the quality of education in low-performing elementary schools, by investing in male college students who aspire to teach young children, thus also providing role models to students who could greatly benefit from them. The program's unique structure allows students to teach and work with individuals over the summer holidays, aiding in their confidence, personal, and professional growth.

Also, during our conversation with Victor Kwansa, a graduate of Yale and Harvard, Kwansa shared his personal experience, stating, "regardless of what school you go to - your colleagues tend to see your skin color first." This is a potent reminder of the realities that individuals of color often face in educational and professional environments, regardless of their credentials or accomplishments.

Yet, in the face of this reality, Kwansa's words also carry an inspiring undertone. They reflect resilience, self-belief, and the courage to continually put one's best foot forward, regardless of the challenges faced. By doing so, we create a space that not only acknowledges our identity but also highlights our skills, passion, and determination.

Access to education should be a universal right. Our guest, former Clerk of Court, Hope Blackley, brought to light the disparity of resources available to students within different zip codes. It's clear that we must advocate for equitable access to resources and opportunities for all students, irrespective of their mailing address.

Furthermore, our discussions have emphasized the need for inclusive and diverse curricula. In a chat with childhood educator DeAnna Lynn, we discussed the transformative power of culturally responsive teaching. According to Lynn, it's essential that students are exposed to a wide range of narratives, not just those of struggle and oppression, but also the stories of trailblazers, creators, history makers, and everyday citizens.

Discipline, as implied by Attorney James Cheek, is another cog in this wheel. Discipline from the inside out, instilling it within our youth, can help them avoid life-altering missteps and detours into the school to prison pipeline. According to the esteemed lawyer, "when you are kicked out of school, you don't have vocational training, your behavior could probably lead to a target on your back - where you end up in prison." Therefore, in addition to advocating for policies and procedures that will reduce unjust burden on minorities, Mr. Cheek encourages students to exemplify good behavior and avoid the pitfalls of being kicked out of school.

Finally, to echo the words of Dr. Nika White, a Diversity, Equity, and Inclusion Consultant, "inclusion is where all the action exists." To truly harness the power of education in promoting racial equity, we must ensure our educational spaces are inclusive, respectful, and welcoming, valuing the diverse perspectives of all students.

Commentary

How exactly can one encourage a more welcoming environment within an educational setting?

This might begin with introspective dialogue, acknowledging our own biases and working to dismantle them. Education should serve as a reflection of our diverse world, accommodating all experiences and histories. It is necessary for educators to foster an environment that not only tolerates but celebrates diversity, thereby instilling a sense of belonging in every student.

A diverse curriculum ensures the inclusion of various perspectives, often overlooked in mainstream education. It encourages critical thinking, empathy, and a broader understanding of the world. It's a stepping stone towards building a more inclusive society, as it allows students from diverse backgrounds to see themselves represented in their learning materials.

Our task includes analyzing the curriculum and admissions process at the institutions that we are familiar with. If there is a lack of diversity, help change it.

Advocate for the inclusion of diverse voices in the curriculum, faculty, and student body. Our active participation can make a world of difference.

Remember, it's up to us to create the change we wish to see.

Reflections:

1. How will you help foster diversity in education and ensure a level playing field?

2. Does the educational institution you're affiliated with have a diverse curriculum?

3. How can you help historically disadvantaged people in their quest to attain higher education?

Mentorship and Community

Mentorship and Community

"We each have a responsibility to leave this world better than we found it." - Mary Thomas

Mentorship and community consistently emerge as powerful tools for positive change.

Mentorship, in its various forms, plays a pivotal role in breaking down barriers, nurturing growth, and empowering individuals. It's about sharing knowledge, fostering personal and professional development, and providing guidance. Mentorship, particularly when mindful of race relations, can offer invaluable support and guidance. It's not merely about teaching a skill or offering career advice; it's about understanding the unique experiences, being a dependable ally, offering support, and empowering individuals to navigate and challenge the systems in place.

Community, on the other hand, provides a sense of belonging, a supportive network where individuals can share their experiences, learn from each other, and work together towards common goals.

In the context of our conversation about race, building inclusive communities can be the first substantial step towards fostering mutual understanding, empathy, and ultimately, equality. When communities are diverse and inclusive, they foster an environment of learning and growth, where empathy becomes organic. They provide a platform where narratives of diverse racial backgrounds are shared, understood, and respected, thus paving the way for mutual respect.

As we continue these conversations about race, it is important to note that mentorship and a sense of community are both a privilege and a responsibility.

Humanity Chats has been privileged to host individuals who have shared about the importance of both mentorship and community. Four such individuals are Mary L. Thomas, Victor Durrah Jr., Councilman Pious Ali, and Dr. Araceli Hernandez-Laroche.

First, let me introduce you to Mary Thomas, the Chief Operating Officer of the Spartanburg County Foundation. Her innovative leadership and commitment to community growth have catalyzed significant advancements in the philanthropy world. Thomas is an epitome of leadership, resilience, and dedication, whose work continually breaks down barriers, especially for women and women of color. Her inspiring journey guides us to utilize our unique talents to bring about positive change. Thomas, a connector, has a special knack for uniting people and nurturing their development.

In one of her most notable accomplishments, Thomas joined forces with a team of eight individuals. Together, they embarked on a transformative journey to establish a village for refugee children in Africa.

Back home in South Carolina, Thomas leads a life of service. She tirelessly devotes her energies to uplift her community, acting as a catalyst for growth and progress. Her efforts have not only resonated with the older generation but have also inspired the young. Thomas' work is a testament to the power of dedicated leadership. She is a mentor to individuals across generations.

Next, we have Victor Durrah Jr., the Founder of BRUH Mentor (Brothers Restoring Urban

Hope). Durrah Jr's steadfast dedication to mentoring urban youth provides them with the necessary tools to navigate and challenge societal structures. He relentlessly strives to uplift and inspire the youth in his community. His nonprofit - BRUH Mentor, is a nonprofit deeply rooted in the ethos of community empowerment. His dedication to group mentorship has sparked a robust platform for instruction and growth, teaching invaluable leadership skills and character development that go beyond the classroom.

His vision extends to fostering an environment of dialogue and thought leadership. BRUH Mentor provides a platform where parents and youth alike can engage in meaningful conversations, challenging preconceived notions and inspiring fresh perspectives. Durrah Jr.'s work resonates profoundly within his community, by demonstrating the profound effect of committed leadership and mentorship.

Next, Councilman Pious Ali, a member of the Maine City Council, who harnesses the power of community. As the first African-born Muslim American elected to public office in the state, his story is one of unwavering commitment to his community. His journey began with Portland Empowered, an organization he founded with the vision of fostering an equitable learning environment. It was during his initial years of service that Councilman Ali was exposed to the harsh realities of inequality. Acting as a quasi parent for immigrant and minority, homeless children, he saw firsthand the stark disparities that these children faced.

Undeterred by these challenges, Councilman Ali embarked on a mission to bridge divides, working diligently to dismantle the 'othering' that existed among kids. Through the Maine Interfaith Youth Alliance, he sought to instill values of unity, understanding, and respect for diversity among the youth. His vision was clear - to foster an environment where kids could learn about humanity and the pivotal role of community service.

In his conversation with us, Councilman Ali emphasized the need to empower the next generation. He firmly believes in nurturing leadership abilities among the young, urging them to actively participate in civic life. It's this belief that underpins his work, driving him to tirelessly advocate for his community. Councilman Ali's story is a powerful reminder of the change that can be brought about when dedicated individuals step up and take action. His impact, both as a community leader and as a public servant, highlights the transformative power of committed leadership.

Lastly, we have Dr. Araceli Hernandez-Laroche, a professor and the founding director of the South Carolina Centro Latino. Her work in academia and the Latino community has continually advocated for inclusivity and mutual respect. Dedicated to public scholarship, she is passionate about bridging the gap between communities and the initiatives meant to support them. Dr. Hernandez-Laroche believes in the power of representation, advocating relentlessly for minorities to have their voices heard and their seats secured at the decision-making table.

A familiar face in her community, Dr. Hernandez-Laroche is a source of inspiration not just for Hispanics/Latinos, but also for women and students. Her work showcases the transformative power of education, active civic participation, and the importance of being seen and heard. Through her actions, she exemplifies what it means to lead by example.

Each of these contributors brings a unique perspective and deep understanding of how mentorship and community can effectively address and improve race relations.

In the narrative of social change, community leaders like Thomas, Durrah Jr., Councilman Ali, and Dr. Hernandez-Laroche are crafting stories of transformation, empowerment, and resilience. As mentors, they embody the foundational principles of Coach, Challenge, Inspire, and Lift Up, empowering us to catalyze positive change in our communities.

Thomas, renowned for her grassroot efforts, exemplifies the act of serving her community.

Victor, with his collaborative projects, echoes the message that progress is a collective effort, urging us not to be paralyzed by fear.

Councilman Ali's tireless advocacy for underrepresented groups epitomizes the principle of 'doing it for the cause and not the applause'. He leverages his position to amplify voices, underlining the importance of representation in policy-making and decision-making processes. His journey teaches us the value of consistency and persistence, urging us to keep going despite challenges.

Dr. Hernandez-Laroche actions emphasize the need to know our purpose.

These leaders challenge us to invest our time, money, and resources into making our communities better, to not give up despite obstacles, and to rise again even if we fail. They inspire us to serve, collaborate, overcome fear, amplify voices, be consistent, and know our purpose. They drive home the message that, together, we can dismantle negative perceptions associated with race.

Their collective wisdom serves as a guiding light, lighting the path for future generations. In the end, their stories are not just about individual accomplishments, but rather a testament to the transformative power of community, mentorship, and committed leadership.

In conclusion, let's take a moment to contemplate the questions on the next page. The answers are not just about recognizing our role in society, but also about understanding how we can contribute to fostering a community that is more inclusive, accepting, and diverse.

Let these reflections ignite a spark within us to become a part of this transformative narrative of change and serve as a guide for self-assessment and growth.

Reflections:

1. Are we investing our time in volunteering for a cause that resonates with our beliefs?

2. Are we making an effort to understand the demographics of our community, to better appreciate the diverse experiences and perspectives it holds?

3. Are our actions empowering a minority? Are we using our influence to give credit to others, inspiring those who look up to us?

Perspective

Perspective

"So far as there is life, there is an opportunity to learn." - Elsie Dickson

Dickson's quote serves as a constant reminder that our journey of learning and growing is ceaseless. Life, in its essence, presents us with endless opportunities to learn, to change, and to become better versions of ourselves. It encourages us to remain receptive to the diverse experiences that life offers and to utilize those experiences as stepping stones towards personal growth and societal progress.

During our Humanity Chat with Social Justice Attorney - Elsie Dickson, she shared profound insights about how our perspective shapes our experiences, beliefs, and interactions. As she passionately discussed, perspective is more

than a viewpoint; it's the lens we use to interpret life.

"Elsie, is your glass half full or half empty?" I asked during our chat, expecting the usual optimistic or pessimistic response. Instead, her answer took me by surprise. She stated that the most important thing was not whether the glass was half full or half empty, but that there was a glass and it had water. This powerful metaphor is a reminder that our ability to perceive and acknowledge the existence of resources, opportunities, or challenges is more crucial than the quantity or proportion.

She then challenged us to think about how we handle the cards life deals us. Can we control it? What led us to our current predicament? What actions are we taking towards a resolution? When confronted with the complex and sensitive *issue of race, these questions take on an even more profound meaning.*

Commentary

In our quest to understand and confront race issues, our perspectives can differ vastly. While some of us may be acutely aware of racial discrimination across the globe, others might be oblivious. Our experiences and background shape our understanding and perception of race.

Perhaps you weren't invited to a party not because of your race but due to other reasons. Or maybe you didn't land the job because there was a candidate with a better qualification.

These examples underscore the importance of considering different perspectives before rushing to judgment. Our perspective not only impacts our life experiences but also influences how we react to situations and events. In navigating race-related issues, let's strive to maintain our composure, be open to different viewpoints, and constantly evaluate and refine our perspectives. After all, it is through understanding and accepting diverse perspectives that we can foster an inclusive, equitable, and empathetic society.

Taking guidance from author M.J Fievre, we can further enrich our perspectives by consciously incorporating a four-step process: evaluating, planning, finding allies, and implementing the change.

Evaluating involves reflecting on our current perspective, acknowledging our biases, and identifying areas for improvement.

Planning entails outlining a strategy to broaden our viewpoint, perhaps by seeking diverse sources of information and experiences.

Finding allies implies seeking those who support and challenge our perspective, fostering growth and understanding.

Lastly, implementing change refers to the active application of our expanded perspective in all interactions and decisions, particularly in conversations about race.

It's essential to reflect on the power of perspective in shaping our life experiences and reactions to events, particularly when dealing with racial matters. Our unique viewpoints, informed by our personal experiences and backgrounds, can either bridge gaps or widen divides. Therefore, it's incumbent upon us to resist the urge to rush to judgments, recognizing that our views are but one piece of a complex puzzle. Let's approach conversations about race with an open heart and mind.

As my mother wisely puts it, "There's your side, my side, and God's side".

Reflections:

1. Are there biases you've identified in your perspective on race? How have these affected your conversations about race?

2. What strategies have you outlined to broaden your perspective on race? Which diverse sources of information or experiences have you sought or plan to seek?

3. Who are the allies you've found who both support and challenge your perspective? How have these relationships contributed to your growth and understanding?

Empathy

Empathy
"With every race, ethnicity, and religion, love is universal, unity is universal, and justice is universal." - R. Valdez McJimpsey

Irrespective of race, ethnicity, or religion, love, unity, and justice are universal principles that bind us all. Empathy, the ability to understand and share the feelings of others, is the key to unlocking these universal principles. As we continue this conversation about race, let's strive to cultivate empathy, bridging cultural and racial divides while promoting unity and justice.

In our Humanity Chat with Valdez McJimpsey, we delved deep into the topics of race, empathy, and the social mandate. McJimpsey, with his experience, shared invaluable insights to help transform our perspective on these vital issues. He emphasized the significance of moving with compassion, sympathy, and empathy, especially when navigating conversations about race.

According to McJimpsey, the experiences he's encountered throughout his life have led him to a profound realization: love, unity, and justice are principles that transcend race, ethnicity, and religion. They are universal tenets that bind us together in our shared human experience. He described empathy as "compassion in motion for others." This paints a beautiful picture of the proactive, intentional nature of empathy – it's not a passive sentiment but an active endeavor to understand and share the feelings of others.

The vision McJimpsey shared with us is one of unity and justice, propelled by love. He believes that when it comes to matters of race, our shared goal should be to foster these three principles. It's a call to each one of us to set our differences aside, embrace empathy, and be more accommodating of each other.

Commentary

Let's take this message to heart as we strive for a world where empathy reigns and our differences serve not as barriers, but as enriching facets of our shared human experiences.

Empathy is not just an emotional response; it's the vehicle that transports us across racial, ethnic, and religious boundaries, offering us a glimpse into the lives, struggles, triumphs, and realities of those different from us. Embracing empathy enables us to see beyond our individual perspectives. By leaning into empathy, we can challenge our biases and broaden our understanding.

Reflections:

1. How can we use empathy as a tool to cross racial, ethnic, and religious boundaries and truly understand the experiences of others who are different from us?

2. In what ways can our personal biases hinder our ability to empathize with others, and how can we confront and overcome these biases?

3. How can fostering empathy within ourselves serve as a catalyst for unity, justice, and societal change?

Faith

Faith

"The church should be a liaison in sharing information." - Bishop Dr. Charles J.J. Jackson

The above quote underscores the profound role of faith communities in bridging gaps, fostering understanding, and promoting dialogue. Just as the dinner table can serve as a place for cross-cultural exchange and understanding, so too can places of worship. They are hubs for community interaction, where individuals from all walks of life can come together, share their experiences, and learn from one another. Faith, in this context, becomes more than just a personal spiritual journey; it evolves into a powerful tool for societal change and unity.

During our Humanity Chat, Bishop Jackson succinctly captured the essence of faith, unity and compassion with his observation that "we are on the same team - we're fighting for the

same cause. Justice for one is justice for all."
These words reverberate with the wisdom and
truth that we so desperately need in our current
times. It's a powerful testament to the unity of
the human spirit, transcending racial and
religious boundaries.

Bishop Jackson's unique insight stems from Dr.
King's teachings, emphasizing the importance
of meeting people where they are. This
approach fosters understanding, compassion,
and empathy, key elements that bridge the gap
between diverse communities. It is through this
understanding that we can truly appreciate the
myriad experiences and perspectives that make
up our shared human tapestry.

The church, according to Bishop Jackson,
should act as a liaison in sharing information.
This role gives it a unique potential to empower,
include, and educate. It's not just about

attending services; it's about ensuring the church is responsive to its members, understanding their needs, and helping them navigate their unique life journeys. The church, in essence, can act as a beacon of hope, inspiring change and fostering unity through its actions and teachings.

The most poignant message I took away from our conversation is the power of love amidst disagreement. Bishop Jackson shared, "We may disagree, but we still have to love." It's a reminder that love and respect should be at the heart of our interactions, regardless of our differences. It's through love that we can foster understanding, bridge divides, and work towards a more harmonious society.

In essence, Bishop Dr. J.J. Jackson's insights serve as a powerful reminder that faith goes beyond personal spiritual journeys. It is a potent tool for societal change, unity, and inclusivity.

Commentary

Whether you follow a religious faith or adhere to personal ethos, your beliefs can serve as a compass guiding your actions towards building a more compassionate, inclusive, and equitable society. As we reflect on our beliefs, let's embrace the power of love, respect, and understanding in our interactions with others.

In conclusion, reflect on how your beliefs guide your actions and attitudes towards others, particularly those who hold different beliefs or perspectives from your own. Also, consider how your spiritual or non-spiritual journeys shape your approach to building bridges and promoting inclusivity.

Reflections:

1. How does your faith or non-faith influence your interactions with others?

2. In what ways does your faith or non-faith inspire you to foster unity and respect in your community?

3. How does your faith or non-faith contribute to your understanding and reactions to societal issues such as inequality and injustice?

Unity

Unity

"If you try, you can find something in common with a lot of people." - Trey Gowdy

This quote reminds us of the shared humanity that binds us, eclipsing our perceived differences. It's a call to encourage dialogue and build bridges of understanding.

In an engaging 'Humanity Chat' session with Former Congressman Trey Gowdy, we delved further into the topic of unity.

Gowdy, a man who wears many hats - a husband, father, author, and prosecutor, shared his unique perspective on unity and the power of relationship-building.

Gowdy's extraordinary journey has been marked by a deep commitment to serving others, having spent several pivotal years advocating for crime victims. He recounts his time in Washington DC, not with the typical tales of political rivalry, but with fond memories of dining with a diverse group of individuals from different political spectrums. These cherished memories, he says, would be his takeaway when he's 95 years old; a testament to his belief in valuing relationships over issues.

Gowdy's affinity for diversity is evident as he skillfully employs a sports analogy to illustrate his stance. Just as we all cheer for different sports teams, our society is comprised of diverse opinions and views. And therein lies our strength. Echoing this sentiment, he insightfully notes, "If all you are doing is talking to people who already agree with you, there are no bridges that need to be built - the bridges have to be built between those of us with different

227

opinions." It is this understanding that drives Gowdy's belief in the power of unity.

The former Congressman astutely remarks, "It's hard to hate up close." The better you know someone, the more difficult it is to marginalize and dehumanize them. His words serve as a poignant reminder that unity is not about uniformity but about embracing and respecting our differences.

In our quest for unity, Gowdy acknowledges the long road ahead in bridging the racial divide. It is a journey that requires time, patience, and understanding. It is a commitment to learn, to grow, and to celebrate our shared humanity, recognizing that beneath our differences, we have much in common.

In the end, Gowdy's words remind us that unity is a journey, not a destination. It is the bonds we forge, the bridges we build, and the understanding we foster that truly define our progress. Let's remember that unity starts with us - with open conversations, genuine connections, and a relentless pursuit of understanding and acceptance.

In our pursuit of unity, the former Congressman offered several actionable steps. First and foremost was the idea of giving everyone a chance. He reminded us that not everyone will get along necessarily, and that's okay. The key is to approach each new interaction without preconceived notions, seeing the slate as blank until the person's actions add or subtract from the relationship.

Living out what we believe in is a powerful means of persuasion. It's about leading by example, embodying the principles we hold dear and letting our actions speak louder than words. Unity, he emphasized, must be prioritized. It calls for a conscious decision not to let differences, particularly those of political nature, poison our relationships and societal harmony.

Being intentional is another crucial aspect. We must not wait for unity to come. Instead, we should proactively seek it out. This means treating everyone the way we would like to be treated. It implies making a deliberate effort to connect with people different from us, in appearance, thought, belief, or religious practice. He noted, "The better you know someone, the more difficult it is to marginalize and not dehumanize that person."

Lastly, the Congressman pointed out an interesting connection between unity and tragedy. If we can find unity before a tragedy strikes, he suggested, we might be able to prevent the next one. This profound thought serves as a call to action for each of us, encouraging us to actively foster unity, understanding, and acceptance in our daily lives.

Commentary

"Diving deeper into the unity discussion, let's not be under the illusion of a faux 'kumbaya' moment, where we blindly accept that everyone will get along peacefully. There are times when comprehending the motivations behind others' actions can be a complex, grueling task.

Take, for instance, why someone would deliberately put an innocent bystander's life at risk by pushing them onto rail tracks, or why an individual chooses to destroy the property of another without any provocation. These acts of violence and aggression are baffling and defy basic human principles of empathy and respect.

Even more perplexing is when race and religion become a target. It's hard to wrap our heads around incidents such as a young white man walking into an African American church and shooting nine church members. The fact that such a heinous crime occurred in a place of worship, where people seek solace, is both heartbreaking and horrifying.

These instances point to a deep-seated problem in our society, a lack of understanding and acceptance of others' differences. It reinforces the importance of our discussions about unity and the need to foster a culture of acceptance.

In the wake of such a chilling event, the grace with which the families of the nine victims handled their grief was nothing short of admirable. They chose the path of forgiveness towards the young white man who had wrought such devastation on their lives. This singular act of mercy not only helped them navigate their grief, but it also served as a guide for the entire State of South Carolina, steering it away from a potentially more tumultuous reaction.

Their act of forgiveness was a testament to the resilience of the human spirit and its ability to rise above hatred and prejudice. It was a clear message of unity, love, and understanding, striking a chord with countless individuals across the nation.

One such person moved by their grace was Tulsi Gabbard, a former congresswoman and a Hindu from Hawaii. Despite hailing from a different faith, Gabbard chose to honor the victims by singing at their memorial at Mother

Emanuel AME church in Charleston. Her homage was not just a tribute to the victims but a powerful reinforcement of the unity that we all need to embrace, regardless of our race or religion.

These remarkable gestures of solidarity and tolerance serve as powerful reminders that unity transcends personal beliefs, race, and backgrounds. It calls on us to extend our empathy and understanding beyond our immediate circles and engage in genuine conversations.

Focusing on our differences or dwelling on the negatives can make finding common ground an uphill task. It's easy to allow our differences - be they racial, religious, or ideological - to create divisions among us. However, the shared human experiences of love, grief, and resilience, as exemplified by the families of the

Charleston victims and figures like Tulsi Gabbard, remind us that unity is not an unreachable ideal, but a choice we can make each day.

Achieving unity may not always be within our grasp. There may be challenges and setbacks along the way. However, by embracing empathy, understanding, and open dialogue, we can navigate the complex nature of human relationships.

A single conversation, a single act of kindness can be a potent catalyst for unity.

As the poet Julia Carney beautifully expressed, "Little drops of water, make the mighty ocean." This underscores the idea that our individual actions, no matter how small they may seem, coalesce to form a substantial impact.

These 'little drops' of dialogue, understanding, and empathy feed into the 'mighty ocean' of social change we aim to achieve. They serve as catalysts, sparking wider discussions about race and challenging ingrained prejudices. It is through these incremental steps that we can gradually dismantle systemic biases and build a society that welcomes unity.

In conclusion, Let's reflect on how we can foster unity and mutual respect in our own spheres of influence.

Reflect on the following questions to deepen your understanding and commitment to unity and actionable change:

Reflections:

1. Is there someone I need to forgive to move forward on my personal journey towards unity?

2. Reflecting on Former Congressman Gowdy's suggestions, how can I actively listen to understand rather than to respond?

3. In what ways can I bring unity and understanding into my personal and professional relationships?

Inclusion and Belonging

Inclusion and Belonging
"We can co-exist as a society by valuing our differences." - Dr. Nika White

Our differences, rather than dividing us, can serve as the foundation for a cohesive society. Recognizing and respecting our differences in race, culture, and experiences is the cornerstone of inclusion and belonging.

In a profound discussion with Dr. Nika White, our conversation was grounded in the principles of unity, respect, and leveraging differences as a strength. Echoing the sentiments of Dr. Martin Luther King Jr., Dr. White reminded us that unity isn't always about agreeing. Rather, it is about a certain level of respect, acknowledging the diverse nature of our human experiences, and cherishing those differences as integral parts of our shared society.

Taking a cue from Dr. King's legacy, we find ourselves in a time ripe with opportunities to influence the circles we belong to. Yes, the challenges can seem daunting but, as Dr. White encouraged us, we must start with our inner circles and expand outward. Our collective desire to create spaces of belonging and unity can fuel transformative change.

Dr. White draws on Dr. King's impact, which serves as a foundation for many Diversity, Equity, and Inclusion (DEI) practitioners today. She notes a pronounced appetite for people to engage in deeper conversations about these issues. The harmful effects of racist tendencies persist, often showing up when least expected. Complacency is not an option. To further this work, we must innovate in our approach, committing ourselves to the trenches rather than sitting on the sidelines.

During our conversation, Dr. White shared that Bryan Stevenson, the Executive Director of the Equal Justice Initiative, advises us to "educate ourselves - get close to the problems." We cannot pretend to understand the depths of these issues from afar. Dr. White urged us to choose courage over comfort, maintaining hope as a crucial catalyst for action.

In our quest for diversity, equity, and inclusion, we must comprehend that diversity spans across many dimensions. We should harness our differences as a source of strength, aiming to produce better outcomes. As Dr. White beautifully articulated, if the ultimate goal is success, it's not about giving everyone a shoe, but rather, a shoe that fits.

Commentary

Our lived experiences shape our perspectives, molding the lenses through which we view and interpret the world. Just as no two fingerprints are identical, no two individuals share identical experiences, and thus, our understanding and interpretation of events vary greatly. These unique experiences, tied to our cultural upbringing, socioeconomic status, education, and personal encounters, molds our perspectives.

However, these differences need not divide us. Instead, they offer an opportunity for us to learn and grow together. Trusting in the process of unification requires us to take small, intentional steps towards common ground. It's about acknowledging and validating the experiences that have shaped our different lenses and using these perspectives to enrich our collective understanding.

Let us remember that progress may often be slow and incremental. The path to societal transformation is seldom linear. However, every step taken, no matter how small, is a step towards our goal. Let's build on the legacy of Dr. King and the wisdom shared by Dr. White to foster a society that is welcoming.

Reflections:

1. Considering your personal journey, in what ways have you experienced or observed both inclusion and exclusion? How have these experiences shaped your understanding of belonging and influenced your perspectives?

2. Reflecting on the environment you find yourself in—be it professional, social, or personal—what proactive steps can you take to foster a greater sense of diversity, equity, inclusion, and belonging?

3. As you think about your future interactions and engagements, how do you envision weaving in the principles of diversity, equity, inclusion, and belonging? What are some specific actions or behaviors you plan to adopt to make this vision a reality?

The New Normal

The New Normal

"Spend time understanding the history of the world." - Lucy Quist

This new normal is not merely a shift in external circumstances; it is an invitation to challenge and transform our most fundamental paradigms. If we are to navigate this transition, we must first understand the history that has shaped our world and the perspectives that have shaped us.

In the past, our understanding of great outcomes was often dominated by conventional measures of success - wealth, prestige, power. However, in the new normal, we are being asked to redefine what great outcomes look like. This is not to say that traditional markers of success are no longer relevant, but rather, they are no longer the only indicators of achievement.

It's important for each of us to reflect on our own journeys. How have our experiences shaped our understanding of welcoming others? How can we use these insights to foster a greater sense of belonging in our environments? Each interaction, each engagement, carries with it the potential to move closer to a more inclusive and understanding society.

We are charting a new course, one that values the richness of our collective experiences and perspectives. It's a journey that requires courage, curiosity, and a willingness to challenge the status quo. Yet, every transformation begins with a single step. In the face of disenfranchisement and an increasingly polarized world, charting a path forward can seem like an insurmountable task. But, as Lucy Quist rightly stated, "we have a collective responsibility to work to change outcomes." The new normal isn't about suppressing our differences, but rather about amplifying them in a way that underscores our shared humanity.

In our schools, workplaces, places of worship, and communities, we need to nurture environments that not only accept but celebrate diversity. The onus is on us to ensure that our fellow humans don't feel disenfranchised. We need to ask ourselves, are we creating spaces where people of all backgrounds feel seen, heard, and valued?

Understanding our present requires us to delve deep into our past. The threads of our history are intricately woven into our current realities, shaping our experiences and perceptions. When we learn about the harsh realities of slavery and oppression, we can begin to understand the systemic injustices that still persist today. By understanding the stories of migration and wars from the past, we can empathize with the struggles of those seeking refuge today.

Our history is teeming with inventors, trailblazers, and pioneers whose stories can inspire us to build on their foundations and strive for more. The knowledge of our origins, our institutional history, is pivotal in shaping our strategies and guiding our path forward.

However, our learning must not be confined to our own cultures or geographical boundaries. If we are truly to foster a global perspective, we need to broaden our horizons.

For instance, if Africa intends to do business with Asia, it becomes pertinent for both continents to understand each other's history, culture, and societal norms. This shared understanding can lay a solid foundation for a prosperous and mutually beneficial future collaboration.

In our quest for a new normal, our goal must be to create a world where we celebrate hard work, innovation, perseverance, as well as diversity, champion equity, and promote an unwavering sense of belonging. This is the journey we must undertake, this is the new normal we must strive for.

Reflection

1. Will you join us in creating a new normal for humanity where your neighbor is positioned for a better outcome?

The Way Forward

The Way Forward

"If you want to change the world, you start at home." - James Cheek

If we aspire to reshape our world into a space, brimming with opportunity, the transformation must begin within our own communities. It's our immediate surroundings that hold the potential for the greatest impact. It's through our everyday interactions, conversations, and actions that we can gradually change underlying attitudes, challenge deep-rooted biases, and pave the way for a harmonious society. This is our call to action - to commence change at our doorstep and let its echo reverberate across the globe.

It's essential that each of us takes a moment to introspect and ask, "Am I doing my part to embrace humanity?" This journey towards belonging demands our active participation - it is only through engagement that we can influence the system to work for all of us. From our dialogues, the necessity of leveraging our platforms and networks to further the movement for progress is clear.

Based on the conversations with the Humanity Chats guests, some of the words that resonate with me are:

- **Love** - Abiding by universal principles that honor every individual's worth.
- **Humility** - Creating a world where respect is both given and received.
- **Embrace** - Building societies where everyone feels accepted.
- **Belong** - Contributing to communities that nurture a sense of belonging.

- **Diversity** - Celebrating not just the similarities, but also the beauty in our differences.
- **Restoration** - Striving towards a world where our shared humanity is restored.
- **Hope** - Dreaming of endless possibilities where everyone thrives.
- **Courage** - Standing up for our beliefs, even when it's challenging.
- **Empowered** - Ensuring everyone has a voice that is heard and respected.
- **Implement** - Taking a firm stand for what is right, and executing it.
- **Unity** - Finding the common thread that links us all, despite our varied backgrounds.

Here are a few actionable steps to promote the vision where we respect and embrace all races:

1. **Educate Yourself and Others** - Learn about systemic biases, their origins, and impacts. Share your knowledge to raise awareness and promote understanding.

2. **Use Your Voice** - Speak up against injustice and discrimination. Your voice has power, use it to influence change.

3. **Support Marginalized Communities** - Actively seek ways to support and uplift communities that have been marginalized.

4. **Challenge Your Own Bias** - Acknowledge and confront your own biases. The first step towards change starts within ourselves.

5. **Promote Diversity and Inclusion** - Advocate for diverse representation in all spaces and ensure everyone feels seen, heard, and valued.

Together with the contributors of this book, we urge you to be that person who helps shape the future. Each action, no matter how small, contributes to the wider movement towards a more equitable and inclusive society. Let us all be the change we want to see in the world.

Together, we can go far.

This has been Humanity Chats' Conversations About Race.

References

Adichie, C. N. (2009, October 7). *The danger of a single story | ted.* YouTube. Retrieved January 26, 2023, from https://www.youtube.com/watch?v=D9Ihs 241zeg

Bowdler, J., & Harris, B. (2022, July 21). *Racial inequality in the United States.* U.S. Department of the Treasury. Retrieved January 26, 2023, from https://home.treasury.gov/news/featured-stories/racial-inequality-in-the-united-stat es

Call me mister is building the next generation of african american male teachers. W.K. Kellogg Foundation. (n.d.). Retrieved January 26, 2023, from https://www.wkkf.org/what-we-do/feature d-work/call-me-mister-is-building-the-next -generation-of-african-american-male-tea chers

Cole, N. L. (2019, June 30). *The difference between Hispanic and Latino.* Courageous Conversation. Retrieved January 26, 2023, from https://courageousconversation.com/the-difference-between-hispanic-and-latino/

Colorism. NCCJ. (n.d.). Retrieved January 26, 2023, from https://www.nccj.org/colorism-0

Hayes, A. (2023, January 12). *What is redlining? definition, legality, and effects.* Investopedia. Retrieved January 26, 2023, from https://www.investopedia.com/terms/r/redlining.asp

Hispanic or Latino origin - census.gov. (n.d.). Retrieved January 26, 2023, from https://www.census.gov/quickfacts/fact/note/US/RHI725221

Hispanic, adj. and n. Oxford English Dictionary. (n.d.). Retrieved January 26, 2023, from

https://www.oed.com/view/Entry/87253?r
edirectedFrom=hispanic#eid

Latino, n. Oxford English Dictionary.
(n.d.). Retrieved January 26, 2023, from
https://www.oed.com/view/Entry/106153?
rskey=ESqpNq&result=1&isAdvanced=fal
se#eid

Marj, M. (2022, December 22). *Humanity
chats with Marjy.* Apple Podcasts.
Retrieved January 26, 2023, from
https://podcasts.apple.com/us/podcast/hu
manity-chats-with-marjy/id1534020084

Merriam-Webster. (n.d.). *Race definition
& meaning.* Merriam-Webster. Retrieved
January 26, 2023, from
https://www.merriam-webster.com/diction
ary/race

Raypole, C. (2021, July 26). *Xenophobia:
Definition, pronunciation, examples, and
more.* Healthline. Retrieved January 26,
2023, from

https://www.healthline.com/health/xenoph
obia

What is racial equity? Race Forward.
(2021, October 5). Retrieved January 26,
2023, from
https://www.raceforward.org/about/what-i
s-racial-equity-key-concepts#:~:text=Raci
al%20equity%20is%20a%20process,live
s%20of%20people%20of%20color.

Wikimedia Foundation. (2023, January
8). *Xenophobia in South Africa.*
Wikipedia. Retrieved January 26, 2023,
from
https://en.wikipedia.org/wiki/Xenophobia_
in_South_Africa

Williamson, E., & Wang, V. (2020, June
2). *'we need help': Coronavirus fuels
racism against Black Americans in China.*
The New York Times. Retrieved January
26, 2023, from
https://www.nytimes.com/2020/06/02/us/
politics/african-americans-china-coronavi
rus.html

CONVERSATIONS ABOUT RACE

Acknowledgements

This book would not be possible without the contributions of our Humanity Chats guests. I am indebted to the 27 guests who shared their knowledge on race with our audience.

Please learn about our contributing guests below:

1. **Dr. Russell Booker** - Retired as Superintendent of Spartanburg County School District Seven following a decades-long service in the district and twenty-eight years in education. Executive Director of the <u>Spartanburg Academic Movement</u> and founder of <u>One Acorn</u>.

2. **Oheneyere Gifty Anti** - An author, entrepreneur, multiple award-winning broadcast journalist, and a

well-respected motivational speaker in Africa and worldwide.

3. **Alicia D. Williams** - Author of several books including *Genesis Begins Again*, which received the Newbery, and Kirkus Prizes, a William C. Morris prize finalist, and won the Coretta Scott King-John Steptoe Award for New Talent.

4. **Dr. Esther Godfrey** - Director of Composition and Professor of Nineteenth-Century British Literature at the University of South Carolina Upstate. She has written extensively on issues of gender, race, and critical aging studies.

5. **Gia Quinones** - Originally from Lima, Peru, Gia Quiñones works at Spartanburg Area Mental Health Center as a school-based mental health

counselor and the Tu Apoyo support line supervisor.

6. **Dr. Araceli Hernadez-Laroche** - A leader of <u>Alianza</u> <u>Spartanburg,</u> Hernandez-Laroche is from Mexico. She is a Professor of Modern Languages and Assistant Chair of the Department of Languages, Literature, and Composition at the <u>University of South Carolina Upstate</u>.

7. **Dr. Begona Caballero-Garcia** - Dr. Begoña Caballero-García is from Spain. An advocate for women, she is an Associate Professor of Spanish Studies and was the Inaugural Dean of Diversity and Inclusion at <u>Wofford College</u>.

8. **Michel Stone** - Author, The Iguana Tree, and Border Child. Border Child received a starred review from Kirkus Reviews and was the lead title on BBC.com's list of 10 recommended books published in April 2017. According to Library Journal Michel's Iguana Tree "recalls the work of John Steinbeck." The book received a starred review from <u>Publishers Weekly</u> and was named a finalist for Foreword Reviews Book of the Year in the multicultural fiction category.

9. **Sumi Mukherjee** - An author and international speaker, his fourth book titled "Minority Viewpoint – my experience, as a person of color, with the American Justice System" was published in Dec 2020.

10.   **Hope Blackley** - A graduate of South Carolina State University, Blackley's many accolades include the Girl Scouts of South Carolina – Mountains to Midlands Woman of Distinction Award. She is a respected community leader and a former Clerk of Court.

11. **Ryan Langley** - A 2002 magna cum laude graduate of Wofford College with a double major in economics and government. After working in the White House during the George W. Bush Administration in 2003, Ryan attended the University of South Carolina School of Law as a Carolina Legal Scholar and a recipient of the Strom Thurmond merit scholarship in law. Langley focuses on cases involving catastrophic injury and/or wrongful death caused by

dangerous/defective drugs and devices, drunk drivers, or medical errors.

12.   **Dr. Walter Lee / Call Me MISTER** - An assistant professor of Middle-Level Education, Dr. Lee is the USC Upstate campus coordinator for Call Me MISTER. He is the faculty advisor of TEACh and the founding leader of Brotherly Conversations.

13.   **LaMonica Okrah** - Growing up in a low-income community, LaMonica always believed there was more in store for her. She never hesitated to take chances. From Chicago to Wall Street and to Harvard Business School, she learned how to break down barriers and move out of her comfort zone.

14. **DeAnna Lynn** - DeAnna Lynn was born in Chicago, IL, and raised in her hometown of Rockford, IL. After attending Rock Valley College and Illinois State University, she began her career of being an Early Childhood Educator.

15. **Tamkara Adun** - Tamkara is a researcher, educator, and Indigenous African historian. Her work focuses on decolonizing African history and shining the light on African indigenous knowledge systems and contributions to global civilization.

16. **James Cheek** - A graduate of the University of South Carolina School of Law, Mr. Cheek was admitted to practice law in 1977. He is a criminal defense

lawyer and a member of the South Carolina State Bar.

17.   **Victor Kwansa** - Received a B.A. in Political Science from Yale University and graduated from Harvard Law School. He is a Blackhouse Foundation Facebook SEEN Black Filmmakers Program Participant, and he was also a finalist for Lena Waithe's 2021 Hillman Grad Mentorship Lab Writing Track.

18.   **Mary Thomas** - Former Chief Operating Officer of the Spartanburg County Foundation and Executive Director of the Robert Hett Chapman Center for Philanthropy. She has over 25 years of experience in the nonprofit sector, is a graduate of <u>Winthrop University</u>, and holds a Bachelor of Arts

Degree in French and Communications. She is a very active leader in the Spartanburg community and has held extensive leadership roles with a host of organizations throughout the area and beyond.

19.   **Victor Durrah Jr.** - A collaborator, leader, and community engagement protagonist, Victor Durrah's mission is to restore and improve his community. A native of Cowpens, Victor Durrah, Jr. is a non-profit leader and has been recognized on numerous occasions for his community work.

20.   **M.J. Fievre** - Born in Port-au-Prince, Haiti, M.J. moved to the United States in 2002. She is the author of the Badass Black Girl series and helps others write

their way through trauma, build community and create social change.

21.   **Valdez McJimpsey** - attended Spartanburg Methodist College and graduated from South Carolina State University with a Bachelor of Science in Psychology. He has done graduate work at Webster University's School of Counseling and is a certified Professional Life Coach through Light University. He is a certified Christian counselor

22.   **Lucy Quist** - The author of 'The Bold New Normal'. She is an international business leader focused on technology, transformation, and thought leadership for positive business returns. The first Ghanaian woman to head a multinational telecommunications company as the

former CEO of <u>Airtel Ghana</u>, she is a co-founder of the <u>Executive Women Network</u> and served as the Vice President of <u>FIFA's normalization committee</u> in Ghana.

23. **Pious Ali** - An assertive, pragmatic, and compassionate leader with a background in community organizing, activism, and civic engagement. Ali is the first African-born Muslim American to be elected to a public office in Maine.

24. **Elsie Dickson** - A Social Justice Lawyer called to the Bar in Ghana and Canada, Dickson works with a community legal clinic providing legal representation to low-income individuals and families in Toronto, Canada. She is a graduate of Wesley Girls' High School,

the University of Ghana - Legon, and the Ghana School of Law. She has a postgraduate diploma in Law from Oxford University, and an LLM from Queen's University, Kingston, Ontario.

25. **Dr. Bishop Charles J.J. Jackson** - A soul-stirring, impactful, passionate preacher and teacher. As an advocate for higher education, Dr. Jackson earned the Bachelor of Arts and Bachelor of Theology degrees from Richmond Virginia Seminary in Richmond, Virginia. In May 2000, he received a Master of Divinity degree from the Samuel DeWitt Proctor School of Theology at Virginia Union University in Richmond, VA. In May 2006, Dr. Jackson earned the Doctor of Ministry degree from Erskine

Theological Seminary in Due West, South Carolina.

26. **Trey Gowdy** - A former state and federal prosecutor, Mr. Gowdy is a family man and a former Congressman, who served as the U.S. Representative for South Carolina's 4th congressional district from 2011 to 2019. Gowdy is an alumnus of Spartanburg High School, Baylor University, and the University of South Carolina.

27. **Dr. Nika White** - She is a national authority and fearless advocate for diversity, equity, and inclusion. As an award-winning management and leadership consultant, keynote speaker, published author, and executive practitioner for diversity and inclusion

efforts across the business, government, non-profit, and education sectors, Dr. White helps organizations break barriers and integrate diversity into their business frameworks.

About the Author

Marjy Marj is a Ghanaian American writer based in South Carolina. After graduating from the Universities of Ghana and Baltimore, she pursued further studies at Duke University. Marjy is the host of Humanity Chats, a show about everyday issues impacting humans. She is the author of The Shimmigrant, Same Elephants,The Young Shimmigrant series, and The Spelling King.

To learn more about Marjy, visit www.marjymarj.com

Thank you for reading.

Other books by the author:

THE
SHIMMIGRANT

MARJY MARJ

CONVERSATIONS ABOUT RACE

CONVERSATIONS ABOUT RACE